PEREGRINE BOOKS

Y19

JANE AUSTEN'S NOVELS

ANDREW H. WRIGHT

ANDREW H. WRIGHT

Jane Austen's Novels

A STUDY IN STRUCTURE

PENGUIN BOOKS
IN ASSOCIATION WITH
CHATTO AND WINDUS

Penguin Books Ltd, Harmondsworth, Middlesex, England
Penguin Books Pty Ltd, Ringwood, Victoria, Australia

—

First published by Chatto & Windus 1953
Published in Peregrine Books 1962
Reprinted 1964

—

—

Made and printed in Great Britain
by Hazell Watson & Viney Ltd
Aylesbury, Bucks
Set in Linotype Pilgrim

FOR

MY WIFE, GINA

CONTENTS

ACKNOWLEDGEMENTS

EVERY student of Jane Austen is grateful to R. W. Chapman for his impeccable and attractive editions of the novels; nor can anyone fail to observe that he is, of all her critics, amongst the most sensible, perceptive, and accurate. And to Miss Mary Lascelles's *Jane Austen and Her Art*, the best single study with which I am acquainted, I must record my profound gratitude for a thousand and one illuminating insights, but most particularly the insights on style. By Marvin Mudrick's *Jane Austen: Irony as Defense and Discovery*, I have been often irritated but always stimulated: his is the best recent study of Jane Austen and represents an encouraging, if sometimes wrong-headed, departure from the usual unpenetrating encomia. If the book were not so unrelentingly patronizing, if Professor Mudrick could occasionally discourage the economic tail from wagging the psychological dog, the book would be vastly better; it stands, even so, as a fresh and original study, very much worth serious consideration.

To those who have given direct help in the preparation of this book I should like also, and more especially, to give thanks. Eliseo Vivas's stimulating lectures on *Pride and Prejudice*, and his challenging suggestions about Jane Austen, have found grateful reflection in the following pages. He taught me what I know about aesthetics; what I do not know, he must not be held accountable for. Murray Krieger, another friend, has with brilliance and tact helped me to correct and sharpen my analysis, particularly in the first chapter.

Miss H. Winifred Husbands has been good enough to read the entire manuscript, and give me the benefit not only of her intimate knowledge of Jane Austen, but of her excellent taste. But to James V. Logan goes the largest measure of gratitude: he saw me through the writing of this book; his relationship to it has been intimate and personal, tireless and brilliant. In common, however, with others who acknowledge their various indebtednesses for the preparation of a book, I must ask that none of those whose names I have just mentioned be blamed for any errors of taste, judgement, or fact which may appear in the following pages. Blame me.

London, June 1952 A.H.W.

NOTE TO THE SECOND EDITION

In the text of this new edition I have made many small changes; those of substance occur for the most part in the sections dealing with *Mansfield Park*, a novel which – thanks to the essays of Charles Murrah and Lionel Trilling – I now understand better than I used to.

The bibliography has been completely revised, and brought up to date.

A.H.W.

London, January 1961

NOTE TO THE 1964 IMPRESSION

Since the second edition went to press, two important books devoted to Jane Austen have been published: Howard S. Babb's *Jane Austen's Novels: The Fabric of Dialogue* (Columbus, Ohio: Ohio State University Press, 1962) contains a series of stylistic analyses of the novels and other works. Ian Watt's compilation, *Jane Austen: A Collection of Critical Essays* (Englewood Cliffs, New Jersey: Prentice-Hall, 1963), contains a valuable survey of Jane Austen criticism by Professor Watt and a brief annotated bibliography, together with critical essays by Kingsley Amis, Reuben A. Brower, Donald J. Greene, D. W. Harding, Arnold Kettle, C. S. Lewis, Alan D. McKillop, Marvin Mudrick, Mark Schorer, Lionel Trilling, Ian Watt, Edmund Wilson, and Andrew Wright.

Three other studies ought to be mentioned: Frank W. Bradbrook's *Jane Austen: Emma* (London: Arnold, 1961), though designed for sixth-formers, contains exceptionally careful and illuminating analyses. Wayne C. Booth's *The Rhetoric of Fiction* (Chicago: University of Chicago Press, 1961) has an excellent chapter on *Emma*. David Lodge's 'A Question of Judgment: The Theatricals at Mansfield Park', *Nineteenth-Century Fiction, XVII* (1962), 275–82, is a further encouraging sign of the reawakened interest in that novel.

A.H.W.

La Jolla, California, January 1964

CHAPTER I

Materials and Themes

JANE AUSTEN occupies an embarrassing position in literary history – embarrassing because never for a moment does she accommodate herself to the facile generalizations which are made about her contemporaries. Wordsworth and Coleridge can, though with some inaccuracy, be called Romantic; they were both born within five years of Jane Austen. But she is too little a writer of the nineteenth century to be called Romantic, too much a person of her time to be called Classic, too original and too great to be considered a precursor or an apotheosis: she is, however much indebted to her literary forebears and coevals, unique. Working with materials extremely limited in themselves, she develops themes of the broadest significance; the novels go beyond social record, beneath the didactic, to moral concern, perplexity, and commitment.

The spinster daughter of a country parson, Jane Austen not only limits herself to the sphere which she understands, she even picks and chooses amongst the raw materials of experience available to her, eschewing what her genius cannot control: '3 or 4 Families in a Country Village is the very thing to work on,' [1] she writes to her niece; but within this narrow range she does not by any means plumb every depth. That she is aware of this fact is evident from her correspondence with James Stainer Clarke, Librarian to the Prince Regent. The story is, though familiar, too significant not to be touched on here.

1. *Letters*, II, p. 401 (to Anna Austen, September 1814). The edition to which I refer here and subsequently is that edited by R. W. Chapman, 2 vols., Oxford, 1952.

In the middle of November 1815, Jane Austen, having a few days previously called at Carlton House and having met the Reverend Mr Clarke, writes him for confirmation of 'my being at liberty to dedicate any future work to H.R.H. the P.R. without the necessity of any solicitation on my part'.[1] His altogether delicious reply contains some suggestions:

Accept my sincere thanks for the pleasure your Volumes have given me: in the perusal of them I felt a great inclination to write & say so. And I also dear Madam wished to be allowed to ask you, to delineate in some future Work the Habits of Life and Character and enthusiasm of a Clergyman – who should pass his time between the metropolis & the Country – who should be something like Beatties Minstrel

Silent when glad, affectionate tho' shy
And now his look was most demurely sad
& now he laughd aloud yet none knew why –

Neither Goldsmith – nor La Fontaine in his Tableau de Famille – have in my mind quite delineated an English Clergyman, at least of the present day – Fond of, & entirely engaged in Literature – no man's Enemy but his own. Pray dear Madam think of these things.

The Reverend Mr Clarke is of course drawing an idealized portrait of himself; Jane Austen replies, in part:

I am quite honoured by your thinking me capable of drawing such a clergyman as you gave the sketch of in your note of November 16th. But I assure you I am *not*. The comic part of the character I might be equal to, but not the good, the enthusiastic, the literary. Such a man's conversation must at times be on subjects of science and philosophy, of which I know nothing; or at least occasionally abundant in quotations and allusions which a woman who, like me, knows only her own mother tongue, and has read little in that, would be totally without the power of giving. A classical education, or at any rate a very extensive acquaintance with English literature, ancient and modern, appears to me quite indispensable for the person who would do any justice to your clergyman; and I think I may boast myself to be, with all possible vanity,

1. This correspondence is contained in full in *Plan of a Novel According to Hints from Various Quarters*, ed. R. W. Chapman, Oxford, 1926, pp. 25–33.

the most unlearned and uninformed female who ever dared to be an authoress.

Readers of Jane Austen will not be deceived by the disclaimers expressed here: she had French and a little Italian; her reading was wide, though she was apparently unfamiliar with the classics; her range extends certainly beyond the comic, as *Mansfield Park* and *Persuasion* definitely show. Yet, despite the misleading humility here, the reader senses the author's perception of her own limitations, so that she deliberately leaves out of her works whatever she cannot personally know and emphasizes what is most malleable to her talent. But Clarke is not yet finished with her; after expressing appreciation for having been sent *Emma*, he writes:

Do let us have an English Clergyman after *your* fancy – much novelty may be introduced – shew dear Madam what good would be done if Tythes were taken away entirely, and describe him burying his own mother – as I did – because the High Priest of the Parish in which she died – did not pay her remains the respect he ought to do. I have never recovered from the Shock. Carry your Clergyman to Sea as the Friend of some distinguished Naval Character about a Court – you can then bring forward like Le Sage many interesting Scenes of Character & Interest.

Nor can he let the matter drop; in the following March he writes again, this time with another suggestion: 'any historical romance, illustrative of the history of the august House of Coburg, would just now be very interesting'. Jane Austen acknowledges both of these letters at once, with a firmness and courtesy that do not, one feels, quite conceal her laughter:

You are very, very kind in your hints as to the sort of composition which might recommend me at present, and I am fully sensible that an historical romance, founded on the House of Saxe Cobourg, might be much more to the purpose of profit or popularity than such pictures of domestic life in country villages as I deal in. But I could no more write a romance than an epic poem. I could not sit seriously down to write a serious romance under any other motive than to save my life; and if it were indispensable for me to keep it up and never relax into laughing at myself or at other people, I am sure I should be hung before I had finished the first chapter. No, I must keep to my own style and go on in my own way, and though I may never succeed again in that, I am convinced that I should totally fail in any other.

And in her *Plan of a Novel According to Hints from Various Quarters* (which Mr Clarke did not see) she releases her hilarity. But behind the laughter is the serious implication that Jane Austen has a firm sense of what materials will be tractable for her; she will not exceed the boundaries she sets herself – the 'little bit (two Inches wide) of Ivory' [1] – and this is the more remarkable when one considers that the most popular novelists of her day deliberately dispensed with the narrow facts of life.

Few of Jane Austen's critics – friendly or unfriendly – have failed to remark her materials, or comment on their adequacy. Nearly every one will agree that within her limits she is superb, but some readers have felt that she is far too circumscribed. It will perhaps be valuable to examine some of the most famous critical dicta, against which we can ask to what degree she limits herself, and how far she is circumscribed.

Scott, one of her earliest and most intelligent admirers, pretty well sums up the case for a generous interpretation in his famous *Quarterly Review* article: '... keeping close to common incidents, and to such characters as occupy the ordinary walks of life, she has produced sketches of such spirit and originality, that we never miss the excitation which depends upon a narrative of uncommon events, arising from the consideration of minds, manners, and sentiments, greatly above our own.' [2] And he very accurately describes the social class to which she limits herself (which it would be superfluous to mention, were it not for the fact that some critics quite misunderstand this fact: see below, p. 22. '[Jane Austen] confines herself chiefly to the middling classes of society; her most distinguished characters do not rise greatly above well-bred gentlemen and ladies; and those which are sketched with

1. *Letters*, II, p. 469 (to J. Edward Austen, 16 December 1816).
2. [Sir Walter Scott,] 'Emma', *Quarterly Review*, XIV (1815), p. 193.

most originality and precision, belong to a class rather below that standard.' [1] Nor does he fail to perceive her merit: 'The author's knowledge of the world, and the peculiar tact with which she presents characters that the reader cannot fail to recognize, reminds us something of the merits of the Flemish school of painting. The subjects are not often elegant, and certainly never grand; but they are finished up to Nature, and with a precision which delights the reader.' [2] Perhaps it does not matter that Scott partly misunderstands Jane Austen (he expresses the opinion in this review that Elizabeth's decision to marry Darcy stems largely from her delight in the elegance of Pemberley), or that he retains a preference for materials intrinsically more romantic – it is indeed the more remarkable that he should genuinely admire her for what she is, and to remark (as he does, eleven years later):

> [I have] read again, and for the third time at least, Miss Austen's very finely written novel of *Pride and Prejudice*. That young lady had a talent for describing the involvements, and feelings, and characters of ordinary life, which is to me the most wonderful I ever met with. The Big Bow-wow strain I can do myself like any now going; but the exquisite touch, which renders ordinary commonplace things and characters interesting, from the truth of the description and the sentiment, is denied to me. What a pity such a gifted creature died so early! [3]

Wordsworth, on the other hand (and as might be expected), while acknowledging the accuracy of her delineations, dislikes them for reasons that readers of the Preface to the *Lyrical Ballads* will find easy to comprehend. Sara Coleridge writes of the admiration with which her father and 'my Uncle Southey' read Jane Austen's novels, '... but Mr Wordsworth used to say that though he admitted that her novels were an admirable copy of life, he could not be interested in productions of that kind; unless the truth of nature were presented to him clarified, as it were, by the pervading light of imagination, it

1. ibid., p. 193.
2. ibid., p. 197.
3. *Journal* (14 March 1826), quoted in Lockhart's *Life*, London, 1837, VI, p. 264.

had scarce any attractions in his eyes'.[1] This is the moderate expression of a dissent which persists (though the terms have changed) to the present day.

Macaulay is neither the first nor the least distinguished commentator to compare Jane Austen to Shakespeare – and, in context, the parallel does not seem strained. 'Shakspeare has had neither equal nor second. But among the writers who ... have approached nearest to the manner of the great master, we have no hesitation in placing Jane Austen, a woman of whom England is justly proud. She has given us a multitude of characters, all, in a certain sense, commonplace, all such as we meet every day. Yet they are all as perfectly discriminated from each other as if they were the most eccentric of human beings.'[2]

On the other hand – and at about the same time – Charlotte Brontë dismisses Jane Austen with considerable disdain. Writing to George Henry Lewes, she asks:

> Why do you like Miss Austen so very much? I am puzzled on that point. What induced you to say that you would have rather written *Pride and Prejudice* or *Tom Jones*, than any of the Waverley Novels?
>
> I had not seen *Pride and Prejudice* till I read that sentence of yours, and then I got the book. And what did I find? An accurate daguerreotyped portrait of a commonplace face; a carefully fenced, highly cultivated garden, with neat borders and delicate flowers; but no glance of a bright, vivid physiognomy, no open country, no fresh air, no blue hill, no bonny beck. I should hardly like to live with her ladies and gentlemen, in their elegant but confined houses. These observations will probably irritate you, but I shall run the risk.[3]

Like Wordsworth, she praises Jane Austen for her accuracy – and like him, she feels in her a want of imagination, though

1. Sara Coleridge, *Memoirs and Letters*, ed. by her daughter, 3rd ed. (London, 1873), I, p. 75 (to Miss Emily Trevenen, August 1934).

2. *The Life and Works of Lord Macaulay*, London, 1866, VII, p. 42 (reprinted from the *Edinburgh Review*, January 1843).

3. Clement King Shorter, *The Brontës: Life and Letters*, London, 1908, I, p. 387 (to George Henry Lewes, 12 January 1848).

the language is different: 'Miss Austen being, as you say, without "sentiment", without *poetry*, maybe *is* sensible, real (more *real* than *true*), but she cannot be great.'[1] A couple of years later she writes to W. S. Williams in much the same vein:

I have ... read one of Miss Austen's works – *Emma* – read it with interest and with just the degree of admiration which Miss Austen herself would have thought sensible and suitable. Anything like warmth or enthusiasm – anything energetic, poignant, heart-felt is utterly out of place in commending these works: all such demonstration the authoress would have met with a well-bred sneer, would have calmly scorned as *outré* and extravagant. She does her business of delineating the surface of the lives of genteel English people curiously well. There is a Chinese fidelity, a miniature delicacy in the painting. She ruffles her reader by nothing vehement, disturbs him by nothing profound. The passions are perfectly unknown to her; she rejects even a speaking acquaintance with that stormy sisterhood. Even to the feelings she vouchsafes no more than an occasional graceful but distant recognition – too frequent converse with them would ruffle the smooth elegance of her progress. Her business is not half so much with the human heart as with the human eyes, mouth, hands, and feet. What sees keenly, speaks aptly, moves flexibly, it suits her to study; but what throbs fast and full, though hidden, what the blood rushes through, what is the unseen seat of life and the sentient target of death – this Miss Austen ignores. She no more, with her mind's eye, beholds the heart of her race than each man, with bodily vision, sees the heart in his heaving breast. Jane Austen was a complete and most sensible lady, but a very incomplete and rather insensible (*not senseless*) woman. If this is heresy, I cannot help it. If I said it to some people (Lewes for instance) they would directly accuse me of advocating exaggerated

1. ibid., I, p. 388 (to the same, 18 January 1848). Perhaps it should be pointed out that Charlotte Brontë's view of imagination is a good deal more limited than Wordsworth's: for her the symptom of imagination is the display of the 'grand passion' – that is, any strong emotion is evidence of imagination; Wordsworth's notion is at once more intellectual and more profound.

heroics, but I am not afraid of your falling into any such vulgar error.[1]

This, one of the most renowned of the attacks ever made upon Jane Austen, deserves an answer. In Miss Brontë's view, Jane Austen's materials are 'the surface of the lives of genteel people'. Certainly the gentry is the material with which Jane Austen works, certainly she avoids the '*outré* and extravagant' in a way that the author of *Jane Eyre* does not – that is, if we are willing to forget Willoughby's letter, Catherine Morland's illusions, William Collins's fatuousness, Aunt Norris's meddling, Mr Elton's charades, and Mrs Clay's scheming. What Miss Brontë confuses is the distinction between dispassion and superficiality: the very calmness with which Jane Austen writes – the 'Chinese fidelity', the 'miniature delicacy' – leads Charlotte Brontë to believe that Jane Austen is an author of the surface only. What she does not see is that in Jane Austen's treatment of her materials there is, by implication, 'that stormy sisterhood' the passions – and a good deal more than 'an occasional graceful but distant recognition' of the feelings. Marianne Dashwood's devotion to Willoughby is fully passionate; so, indeed, is Anne Elliot's to Captain Wentworth – and does not Emma reproach herself for her want of 'tenderness of heart'? But what Miss Brontë overlooks entirely – even if we leave out the passions and the feelings – is Jane Austen's moral concern, her fervent preoccupation with the way people behave; and her '3 or 4 Families in a Country Village' no more limit her than the Danish nobility confines Shakespeare in *Hamlet*.

If Charlotte Brontë is understandably unfair, Edward FitzGerald is deliberately testy about Jane Austen: he finds her 'quite capital in a Circle I have found quite unendurable to walk in'. In his references to her, scattered through his letters, he complains that 'she never goes out of the Parlour . . .' and again, 'I cannot get on with Books about the Daily Life which I find rather insufferable in practice about me. I never could

1. Clement King Shorter, *The Brontës: Life and Letters*, London, 1908, II, pp. 127, 128 (to W. S. Williams, 12 April 1850).

read Miss Austen, nor (later) the famous George Eliot. Give me People, Places, and Things, which I don't and can't see; Antiquaries, Jeanie Deans, Dalgettys, etc. ...'[1] As he 'could not read Miss Austen', perhaps he never came across Elizabeth Bennet's famous remark to her sister: '"The more I see of the world, the more am I dissatisfied with it; and every day confirms my belief of the inconsistency of all human characters, and of the little dependence that can be placed on the appearance of either merit or sense."'[2] It is just her dissatisfaction with the daily life that she finds around her that enables Jane Austen to examine it so minutely. That she 'never goes out of the Parlour' is, hyperbolically at least, true. H. W. Garrod makes a similar complaint: 'A drab scenery the worse for use; a thin plot unfashionably cut, and by turning, relining, and trimming made to do duty for five or six novels; a dozen or so stock characters – these are Miss Austen's materials.'[3] But those who find in Jane Austen's materials nothing adequate for the exposition of great themes run the risk of placing themselves on the level of Humberstall, the Cockney mess-waiter in Kipling's famous story. Speaking of Jane Austen's novels (which he read to please his officers), he says:

''Twasn't as if there was anythin' *to* 'em either. *I* know. I had to read 'em. They weren't adventurous, nor smutty, nor what you'd call even interestin' – all about girls o' seventeen (they begun young then, I tell you), not certain 'oom they'd like to marry; an' their dances an' card-parties, an' picnics, and their

1. *Letters*, London, 1894, II, p. 13 (to W. F. Pollock, 23 February 1860); II, p. 131 (to the same, 24 December 1871); II, p. 190 (to S. Laurence, 30 December 1875).

2. *Pride and Prejudice*, p. 135. All my citations of Jane Austen's novels are from the edition of R. W. Chapman, 5 vols., 3rd ed., Oxford, 1933.

3. H. W. Garrod, 'Jane Austen: a Depreciation', in *Essays by Divers Hands, Being the Transactions of the Royal Society of Literature of the United Kingdom*, n.s., VIII (1928), pp. 36, 37. For a stinging rebuttal to this attack, see R. W. Chapman, 'Jane Austen: a Reply to Mr Garrod', ibid., n.s., X (1931) pp. 17–34.

young blokes goin' off to London on 'orseback for 'air-cuts an' shaves.' [1]

In short, nearly all Jane Austen's readers – admirers and detractors alike – see in her choice of subject matter a deliberate limitation, a smallness of range. But those who like her find her scope quite adequate to the exposition of important themes; those who dislike her complain that the country gentry cannot possibly yield anything of surpassing value. We must, then, turn to Jane Austen's themes, their nature and validity: and perhaps it will be prudent in this connexion to examine what other critics have said on the subject.

There is, surprisingly enough, a school of critics who think that Jane Austen's text is money. Logan Pearsall Smith finds *Pride and Prejudice* 'both didactic and mercenary', though he does not develop this point. Perhaps, like Scott, he forgets Charlotte Lucas, or actually believes Elizabeth when she says that she fixed upon Darcy after seeing the elegance of Pemberley.[2] Leonard Woolf, writing in 1942 on what he calls the 'Economic Determinism of Jane Austen', alleges that her 'social and economic standards ... [are], except in one important particular [she is against 'work': her heroes, he says, do not work], those which we associate with a capitalist bourgeoisie rather than with country gentlemen and aristocrats. ... The social standards are almost entirely those of money and snobbery. It is remarkable to what an extent the plots and characters are dominated by questions of money.' [3] Such a position can be taken only if the novels are misread; as one of the editors of *Notes & Queries* so economically puts it, in reply to Mr Woolf: 'Whose standards? Jane's or her characters'?' [4] But Mr Woolf is not the only critic to misinterpret

1. Rudyard Kipling, 'The Janeites', *Debits and Credits*, London, 1926, pp. 156, 157.

2. Logan Pearsall Smith, 'On Re-Reading Jane Austen', *New York Evening Post Literary Review* (8 March 1924), p. 574. This does not, however, represent his opinion as to the entire canon.

3. Leonard Woolf, 'The Economic Determinism of Jane Austen', *New Statesman and Nation*, XXIV (1942), p. 40.

4. *Notes & Queries* (15 August 1942), p. 91.

Jane Austen's attitude to money. In one of the most extraordinary pieces ever written on Jane Austen, David Daiches says that Jane Austen is 'the only English novelist of stature who was in a sense a Marxist before Marx. She exposes the economic basis of social behaviour with an ironic smile. . . .' And he continues, by way of amplification: 'Critics have remarked that there is no real delineation of true love in Jane Austen, and that is true enough, for Miss Austen knew only too well that in that kind of society genteel young ladies cannot afford true love: their objective must be marriage, and marriage with someone *eligible*. In Jane Austen, only the poor can afford passion.' [1] To those who take seriously such criticism, Dr Chapman reminds us of 'Elizabeth's repudiation of Collins, Fanny's of Crawford, Anne's of her crafty cousin. Their words are not less eloquent than their actions: Marianne's, when she contemns Colonel Brandon's advancing years and flannel waistcoats; Elizabeth's when she censures her friend's calculating prudence; Anne's when she claims for her sex "the privilege . . . of loving longest when existence or when hope is gone".' [2]

And there is a group of critics who allege that Jane Austen has no moral concern. Léonie Villard is among them. 'Merely an amused and attentive spectator, Jane Austen does not seek to interpret life, she is content to observe it, but her mind and her sentiments are always in unison with the objects of her observation.' [3] Thus interpreted, Jane Austen's novels are

1. David Daiches, 'Jane Austen, Karl Marx, and the Aristocratic Dance', *American Scholar*, XVII (1948), pp. 289, 290. Professor Daiches is in this essay indulging in a joke which I did not at first see. What he meant ironically, I read straightforwardly. But perhaps it will be allowable to say here (what Professor Daiches already knows) that Jane Austen's major concern is with the gentry, which disliked the aristocracy. See R. W. Chapman, *Jane Austen Facts and Problems*, Oxford, 1948, pp. 26, 198, 199.

2. R. W. Chapman, *Jane Austen Facts and Problems*, pp. 192, 193. Compare Mark Schorer, 'Fiction and the "Matrix of Analogy" ', *Kenyon Review*, XI (1949), pp. 539–44.

3. Léonie Villard, *Jane Austen: a French Appreciation*, translated by Veronica Lucas, New York, 1924, p. 191.

merely the detached record of some commonplace incidents amongst the gentry of her time and place. Professor Mudrick makes amorality central to Jane Austen's irony:

> Her earliest, and always her characteristic, defense is irony: throughout her letters and extravagantly in her *juvenilia*, she observes and defines, without moral or emotional engagement, the incongruities between pretense and essence, between the large idea and the inadequate ego. Here, indeed, irony becomes for her a positive agent and appears as the only possible interpreter of life. Later . . . she turned away from irony more and more often to her alternative defense, convention, until her grand – though temporary – apostasy from irony in *Mansfield Park*. . . . Her temperament chose irony at once: she maintained her distance by diverting herself and her audience with an unengaged laughter, by setting irony, the instrument – and, as it happened, the genius – of her temperament, to sharpen and expose all the incongruities between form and fact, all the delusions intrinsic to conventional art and conventional society.[1]

But all art is necessarily concerned with morality (though music, as usual, poses unique problems here), because all art must deal with man's actions in the world. This is not to argue that art's single, or even principal, function is that of a criticism of life. But every work of art is, willy-nilly, such a criticism, whether we consider the stern morality of a Henry James, or the profound immoralities of a Stendhal. It is therefore begging the question to call a novel amoral; and, as I hope to show, irony is the instrument of a moral vision, it is not a 'technique of rejection'.

Jane Austen, then, must have a scheme of values which can be inferred from her works. Even her detractors are generally willing to admit this fact; Mr Garrod complains:

> It would be difficult to name a writer of similar eminence who possessed so little knowledge of literature and history, whose experience of life was so narrowly and contentedly confined, whose interests were at once so acute and so small, whose ideals were so

1. Marvin Mudrick, *Jane Austen: Irony as Defense and Discovery*, Princeton, 1952, p. 1.

irredeemably humdrum . . . a just irritation is constantly aroused in me by the monotonously subdued pitch of her ethical standards. . . . Her experience, her interests, her morality, her education, were precisely those of any other young woman of her time and place.[1]

Lord David Cecil, though he admires Jane Austen extravagantly, regards her as a kind of apotheosis of her father's *Zeitgeist*. 'Like all great comedians, she satirizes in relation to a universal standard of values: her books express a general view of life. It is the view of that eighteenth-century civilization of which she was the last exquisite blossom. One might call it the moral-realistic view.'[2] And Elizabeth Bowen provides a third example of the group of critics which regards Jane Austen as having a rigid and conventional sense of values. 'She lived, it is true, in a small and very secure world, in which values were not questioned: nothing got dragged up. Her unperplexity – or the resentment it arouses – is perhaps at the root of many objections to her.'[3] So to regard Jane Austen is palpably to ignore the period in which she lived: but, far more important, such a view oversimplifies the themes of the novels themselves.

Her period, of course, was that of the first generation of Romantic poets, of the French Revolution, and the War of American Independence; of Malthus, Wordsworth, Fichte, Scott, Schelling, Hegel, Coleridge, Napoleon, Andrew Jackson, William Wilberforce – and even James Fenimore Cooper. It might be argued, however, that country life in her part of the world was relatively undisturbed, even then. Physically, it is true, her life was lived much as it might have been fifty years previously – but she could not be so anachronistic as to ignore the *Zeitgeist* or the great events of her time. She had two brothers in the Royal Navy (they both eventually became admirals), she had close family connexions with Warren

1. H. W. Garrod, op. cit., pp. 29, 30.

2. Lord David Cecil, 'Jane Austen', in *Poets and Story-Tellers, A Book of Critical Essays*, London, 1949, p. 115.

3. Elizabeth Bowen, 'Jane Austen: Artist on Ivory', *Saturday Review of Literature*, XIV (15 August 1936), p. 3.

Hastings, and a cousin whose *émigré* husband was guillotined in the Terror. And almost every reader of hers will know of her familiarity with Godwin, Goethe, Wordsworth, Scott, Southey, Byron – by none of whom was she untouched: writing to her sister from Bath, Jane Austen says that a Mr Pickford 'is as raffish in his appearance as I would wish every Disciple of Godwin to be'. *Love and Freindship* is partly modelled after *The Sorrows of Young Werther*, to which she makes satiric reference in her burlesque. In *Sanditon*, one of the silliest characters declares that Wordsworth has '"the true soul"' of poetry, and of Scott's '"beautiful Lines on the Sea"': '"That Man who can read them unmoved must have the nerves of an Assassin! Heaven defend me from meeting such a Man un-Armed."' She shows in her letters her familiarity with Southey, whose 'Poet's Pilgrimage to Waterloo' she thinks 'very beautiful' in parts. Byron comes into consideration in *Persuasion*, when Captain Benwick and Anne discuss literary matters.[1] In any event, her world was not – it could not be – that of Squire Allworthy and Uncle Toby.

But, as some have contended, she might simply have held to the past, have rejected the present and its implications. Then her themes might reflect or embody the morality of her father's generation. If so, a man like Mr Garrod might more reasonably complain of her 'humdrum ideals'; or a more friendly critic like Lord David Cecil might convincingly speak of her as 'the last exquisite blossom' of the eighteenth century. Bradley speaks of her 'moralizing tendency' and sees in her work a close connexion to Dr Johnson.[2] Actually, however, it

1. *Letters*, I, p. 133 (to Cassandra Austen, 21 May 1801); *Love and Freindship and Other Early Works*, London, 1922, p. 24; [*Sanditon*,] *Fragment of a Novel*, Oxford, 1925, p. 89. (There are many other allusions to Scott. See *Sense and Sensibility*, pp. 47, 92; *Mansfield Park*, pp. 86, 281; *Persuasion*, pp. 100, 107, 167; *Letters*, I, pp. 197, 248; II, pp. 290, 300, 404, 431, 432, 433, 468); *Letters*, II, p. 476 (to Alethea Bigg, 24 January 1817: compare *Letters*, I, p. 212; II, p. 345); *Persuasion*, pp. 100, 107, 167 (compare *Letters*, II, p. 379).

2. A. C. Bradley, *Essays and Studies by Members of the English Association*, II (1911), pp. 14–17.

is just her moral complexity which gives sharpness to her themes. Johnson himself held to a rigorous orthodoxy in politics, in religion, and in his social ideas: but even he admitted more scepticism than he perhaps knew, in 'The Vanity of Human Wishes', the last few lines of which cannot efface the Ecclesiastes-like tone of what has gone before. Jane Austen, though without any vehement renunciations, looks at man in the world and is deeply troubled by what she sees: a coarse and inadequate world with coarse and inadequate standards – but she can neither abandon the world nor wholly reject its standards; she sees men and women as silly but kind, attractive yet wicked, vain and vexing; laughable, pretentious, deluded, stupid; but deeply human, often intelligent, and – above all – capable of love. She is no narrow expositor of an outworn morality, no mere angry satirist: 'Her object is not missionary,' as D. W. Harding points out; 'it is the more desperate one of merely finding some mode of existence for her critical attitudes.' [1]

The novels can, I think, be considered on three levels of meaning: first, the purely local – that is, they can be looked at as illustrative of country life among the upper middle classes in southern England at the end of the eighteenth century. Second, they can be taken as broad allegories, in which Sense, Sensibility, Pride, Prejudice, and a number of other virtues and defects are set forth in narrative form and commented on in this way. Third, there is the ironic level, and if Jane Austen's novels be considered in this light, then one can regard the various incidents, situations, and characters as implying something beyond what they embody, as symbolic rather than allegorical. There is, of course, nothing new in all this: all great art is universal, just as in some ways it is illustrative of the time in which it was created. But I set forth these categories to prevent, or rather to unscramble, the confusion in which Jane Austen criticism finds itself.

If a novel is social history and nothing else, then we should

1. D. W. Harding, 'Regulated Hatred: an Aspect of the Work of Jane Austen', *Scrutiny*, VIII (1940), p. 351.

no doubt abandon literature for the more comprehensive and factual accounts of the historians and the sociologists. Jane Austen, as both her admirers and detractors point out, gives by no means a full picture of even the narrow segment of society which is portrayed in the six novels. And what a narrow segment it is. She quite definitely omits to consider the lower classes: servants appear wherever servants are necessary; at Mansfield, at Hartfield, even at Barton Cottage and in Portsmouth; but they are barely seen, and almost never heard. We are told that Emma is kind to the poor, but there is no exchange of conversation disclosed to us. Even the yeomanry is kept almost entirely out of sight: Robert Martin does not utter a syllable, and the important letter which he writes to Harriet Smith is not printed, it is only discussed; Emma catches a glimpse of him, but at a distance. As for the aristocracy, Jane Austen hardly touches on it; but when she does, its members are usually satirized. Lady Catherine de Bourgh is the daughter of an earl, but her arrogant and pretentious stupidity evokes our measured disdain; the Honourable John Yates is the high-living and low-thinking companion of young Tom Bertram and the one who suggests performing *Lovers' Vows* at Mansfield – that is, he is inconsiderate, insensitive, and silly; the Dowager Viscountess Dalrymple and her daughter are, in Anne Elliot's devastatingly adequate word, 'nothing'; Colonel Fitzwilliam, it is true, is unexceptionable, but he is flat, a functional character who exists mostly to buttress Elizabeth's pride by telling her of Darcy's part in breaking up the attachment between Bingley and Jane.

So we are left with the country gentry, if (like Jane Austen) we occasionally include in this class such people as the Coles and Mr and Mrs Gardiner. But even the gentry is not portrayed in all its aspects. For one thing, there is very little religion in the novels: piety, yes, but no deep spiritual insights, no theological speculations. Jane Austen does not even suggest the reactions on her characters of the great events of the day (if we except Sir Walter Elliot's reaction to 1814 – he decides to consider renting Kellynch to a sailor). There is hardly any hunting or shooting, though it is mentioned in four of the novels. Men do not appear, except in the company of women.[1] Politics are eschewed: when Catherine Morland and Henry Tilney commence to talk on the subject, 'it was an easy step to silence'. And in fact all that is related is of the ordinary social intercourse of the gentry, with the emphasis on women. As sociology or as history, therefore, the novels are neither comprehensive nor adequate within the small sphere they do include; and Jane Austen's greatness can hardly rest on her competence in this area. Let us then turn to the didactic level.

On this level, *Sense and Sensibility* is an instructive treatise in which Sensibility is portrayed as a dangerously excessive attribute and Sense as a moderate, laudable, and worthy aim. Marianne Dashwood's ardent enthusiasm leads to heartbreak, disillusion, misery, despair – and to marriage with a colourless man well beyond his first youth. Elinor's intelligent self-control does not keep her from disappointment and sadness, but it supports her in moments of dejection just as it precludes the violence of rapture; and she is rewarded by a marriage of love to an earnest and stolid but affectionate young clergyman. Thus considered, the book centres around two quite abstractable human predispositions; the moral is that Sense is more than its own reward, Sensibility less than its own promise.

Indeed a curious paradox of a 'rational' age is its sentimental effusions, unless one chooses to regard the eighteenth century's view of the mind, its faith in the ability of the reason to grapple successfully with every problem, as sentimental. At any rate, sensibility as a mode of life had already, by Jane Austen's time, gained wide acceptance, at least in literary convention.

Dear sensibility! source inexhausted of all that's precious in our joys, or costly in our sorrows; thou chainest thy martyr down

1. So far as I can discover, W. F. Pollock was the first critic to remark this fact, in 'British Novelists: Richardson, Miss Austen, Scott', *Fraser's Magazine*, LXI (1860), p. 31.

upon his bed of straw, and 'tis thou who lift'st him up to HEAVEN. Eternal fountain of our feelings! 'tis here I trace thee, and this is thy *'divinity which stirs within me'*; not that in some sad and sickening moments, *'my soul shrinks back upon herself, and startles at destruction'* – mere pomp of words! – but that I feel some generous joys and generous cares beyond myself; all comes from thee, great, great SENSORIUM of the world! ...[1]

Such an apostrophe (though one might regard Sterne as having his tongue in cheek here) requires an answer, just as Goldsmith's *Deserted Village* must be balanced by Crabbe's *Village*. (Certainly it is not inapposite to mention Crabbe here, for he was one of Jane Austen's favourites; writing to her sister after hearing of Mrs Crabbe's death, she says: 'Poor woman! I will comfort *him* as well as I can, but I do not undertake to be good to her children. She had better not leave any.' [2])

So *Sense and Sensibility* can be read as a vindication of Sense, as a comic treatment of Sensibility. *Northanger Abbey* is equally susceptible of a didactic interpretation: it is, for the most part, a burlesque of the Gothic novel of terror, with special reference to Ann Radcliffe's *Mysteries of Udolpho*. Catherine Morland is, in Marvin Mudrick's words, the 'anti-type' of the Gothic heroine: she is an ordinary, plain-faced, rather prosaic girl of unmysterious origin. Miss Lascelles quite succinctly contrasts her to Charlotte Smith's Emmeline:

Emmeline ... had 'of every useful and ornamental feminine employment ... long since made herself mistress without any instruction'. But Catherine, alas, 'never could learn or understand any thing before she was taught; and sometimes not even then, for she was often inattentive, and occasionally stupid'. And whereas Emmeline 'had learned to play on the harp, by being present when Mrs Ashwood received lessons on that instrument', *she*, at the height of her career as heroine, had advanced no farther than to be able to 'listen to other people's performance with very little fatigue'. This was not all – 'her greatest deficiency was in the

1. Laurence Sterne, *A Sentimental Journey through France and Italy* ... London, 1949, p. 150.

2. *Letters*, II, p. 358 (to Cassandra Austen, 21 October 1813).

pencil'; here she fell miserably short of Emmeline, who 'endeavoured to cultivate a genius for drawing, which she inherited from her father'. It is true that, 'for want of knowing a few general rules, what she produced had more of elegance and neatness than correctness and knowledge', but when this small defect had been remedied by a friend's communication of these few general rules, she was able to execute a faultless portrait of her Delamere ... while poor Catherine, her looking-glass image and opposite, 'had no notion of drawing – not enough even to attempt a sketch of her lover's profile, that she might be detected in the design'.[1]

And on one level the novel tells the story of her gradual awakening from the Gothic dream, her growing realization that the world is more sensible than she has believed it to be. The enlightenment comes after she has crept to the deceased Mrs Tilney's bed-chamber, half expecting to find the poor woman 'shut up for causes unknown, and receiving from the pitiless hands of her husband a nightly supply of coarse food'.[2] Instead, she sees a large, neat, sunny room – and she is caught there by Henry Tilney, who satisfies her that his mother has died from quite natural causes.

Her thoughts being still chiefly fixed on what she had with such causeless terror felt and done, nothing could shortly be clearer, than that it had been all a voluntary, self-created delusion, each trifling circumstance receiving importance from an imagination resolved on alarm, and every thing forced to bend to one purpose by a mind which, before she entered the Abbey, had been craving to be frightened. She remembered with what feelings she had prepared for a knowledge of Northanger. She saw that the infatuation had been created, the mischief settled long before her quitting Bath, and it seemed as if the whole might be traced to the influence of that sort of reading which she had there indulged.[3]

1. Mary Lascelles, *Jane Austen and Her Art*, London, 1939, p. 60.

2. *Northanger Abbey*, p. 188. Compare *The Mysteries of Udolpho*, chap. 29: '... he continued to confine her in the turret, under a strict guard; and, without pity or remorse, had suffered her to lie, forlorn and neglected, under a raging fever, till it had reduced [her] to the present state'. Quoted by Dr Chapman in an appendix to his edition of the novel, p. 285.

3. *Northanger Abbey*, pp. 199, 200.

And that is that – on the didactic level. Thus also *Pride and Prejudice* displays and illustrates the dangers of excessive Pride and overweening Prejudice: what 'happens', in part, in the novel is that Darcy becomes decreasingly proud – compare his second proposal of marriage to the first; and that Elizabeth becomes proportionately less prejudiced – compare her haughty first reaction to Darcy's letter and the sweet pertness of her behaviour when at last she accepts him. In fact the choice and arrangement of the main and complementary characters is such as to underscore this interpretation. Bingley and Darcy are sharply contrasted from the very beginning – the former has 'a pleasant countenance, and easy, unaffected manners', the latter, a 'fine, tall person, handsome features, noble mien . . . [but] he was discovered to be proud . . .' Bingley is remarkable for 'easiness, openness, ductility of . . . temper', while Darcy is 'haughty, reserved, and fastidious, and his manners, though well bred, were not inviting'.[1] Similarly with Jane and Elizabeth: Miss Bennet is a 'regular' beauty, while Darcy observes in the younger sister 'more than one failure of perfect symmetry'. Jane's manner is reflected on by her sister, after receiving the letter from Darcy: 'Jane's feelings, though fervent, were little displayed, and . . . there was a constant complacency in her air and manner, not often united with great sensibility'.[2] Elizabeth, on the other hand, is pert and lively. But to go no further in analysing the book is to do it manifest injustice.

And whereas it is impossible to be satisfied with so shallow an interpretation of *Pride and Prejudice*, the theme of *Mansfield Park* is all too plainly limited to the didactic: it is a treatise on education. As Dr Chapman says:

> The ostensible moral of the book, which is almost blatantly didactic, is that education, religious and moral, is omnipotent over character. It is true that this theory is oftenest voiced by the more priggish of the persons; solemn Sir Thomas, his virtuous son, and his pensive niece. But it is plainly endorsed by their author, who

1. *Pride and Prejudice*, pp. 10, 16. 2. ibid., pp. 23, 208.

was perhaps at this time too much under the influence of one of her favourite divines or secular moralists.[1]

Nor does the novel ever go beyond this plane: there is no conflict within Fanny's nature. To be sure, *Mansfield Park* is an extraordinarily honest book: Fanny is not always inhumanly good as some critics have said; for she does feel deeply hurt when Edmund lets Mary Crawford ride the pony reserved for her own use; she has moments of jealousy when she must view the rehearsal of Edmund and Mary doing a love scene from the play; she is appalled by the vulgarity of her own father, and by the slatternliness of her mother, at Portsmouth. So Fanny is not sentimentalized – or at least not so much so as is the heroine of *Evelina*. But neither is Fanny, or her book, deep.

As a novel of instruction, *Emma* centres around the faults of the heroine: she is spoiled and conceited. And in the course of the book, through the frustration of her self-confident efforts to play God, she learns better. She is always wrong but always thinks she is right. She imagines that she can marry Harriet off to Mr Elton, but not only does she mistake the vicar's character (she thinks him ambitious to marry for love and nothing else), she mistakes his evidences of affection – thinks Harriet is the object when she herself is the real goal. Emma is quite easily misled by Frank Churchill – twice misled, for she believes him when he complains of Jane Fairfax, and persuades herself that he is in love with her. She is even wrong in her analysis of her own feelings toward Mr Knightley; she must be shocked by Harriet's 'pretensions' in that direction, before she can bring herself to an acknowledgement that she loves him. *Emma* is, considered in this light, a drawing-room comedy of Self-Deception; the gradual disclosure of the heroine's misapprehensions is as amusing as it is inevitable. On this level, the book is, as an early reviewer puts it, an 'inoffensive and well principled novel'.[2]

In the same way, the theme of *Persuasion* is Overpersuasion. The stuff of the book is made of Anne Elliot's ill-advised

1. R. W. Chapman, *Jane Austen Facts and Problems*, p. 194.
2. *British Critic*, n.s., VI (1816), p. 96.

refusal of Frederick Wentworth when, as a girl of nineteen, she was persuaded that he was unacceptable as a husband. And what happens is that Anne almost loses him for ever; it is a set of very fortunate (and fortuitous) circumstances – the renting of Kellynch to his sister's husband, his own remarkable success in the Navy, the fall of Miss Musgrove at Lyme – that finally brings them together again. A tart, pompous, and superficial early reviewer laments the moral of the book, 'that young people should always marry according to their own inclinations and upon their own judgement . . .' [1]

Almost no one today, however, can be satisfied to read Jane Austen's novels so superficially. But what lies beneath the stylized surface of these books? Is their author merely a genial miniature painter, whose very malice is tinged with warm-hearted good sense? Is Jane Austen as unlearned and as naïve as she claims to be? Is she composed, shallow, banal? Is she 'merely an amused and attentive spectator', or a great deal more? My argument will be that Jane Austen's novels are too complex to allow a merely didactic interpretation, too serious to be dismissed as simply light-hearted: 'she contemplates virtues, not as fixed quantities, or as definable qualities, but as continual struggles and conquests, as progressive states of mind, advancing by repulsing their contraries, or losing ground by being overcome.' [2]

Indeed, it is possible to go further: it is possible to say that Jane Austen's themes are ironic. And here I must digress, for discourse is not yet sufficiently universal to permit the use of the term 'irony' without some explanation. My intention is to apply the term to a world view, as the juxtaposition, in fact, of two mutually incompatible views of life.[3] Irony is an existential determination,' says Kierkegaard, 'and nothing is more ridiculous than to suppose that it consists in the use of a cer-

1. *British Critic*, n.s. IX (1818), p. 301.

2. 'Jane Austen', *North British Review*, LII (1870), p. 137.

3. There is ample historical justification for so considering irony. See my paper, 'Irony and Fiction', *Journal of Aesthetics and Art Criticism*, XII (1953), 111–18.

tain phraseology, or when an author congratulates himself upon succeeding in expressing himself ironically. Whoever has essential irony has it all day long, not bound to any specific form, because it is the infinite within him.'[1]

Of the contradictions in human experience, Jane Austen has a perception which yields a detachment, and a detachment which grants a perception. There is, in her disengagement, an objectivity which is not scientific, because not disinterested. In fact she is deeply concerned with both aspects of the contradictions she perceives: searching the orchards of human experience she finds the bitter-sweet fruit of confusing appearance and ambiguous essence – and she becomes a person of the divided, the ironic vision.

But this view of irony raises some issues which require explanation. Thus Professor Chevalier (writing, it must be admitted, on Anatole France) asserts that 'the basic feature of every Irony is a contrast between a reality and an appearance.'[2] But the matter is not so simple: the ironist is not sure which is and which merely seems. Who, for instance, would dare say that Don Quixote's tragic and lovable 'illusions' are only appearance and that the real world is that of Sancho Panza? How, then, are we to judge the issues involved? Professor Chevalier's answer is that irony is 'a mode of escape from the fundamental problems and responsibilities of life'.[3] More specifically, he says, 'Irony characterizes the attitude of one who, when confronted with the choice of two things that are mutually exclusive, chooses both. Which is but another way of saying that he chooses neither. He cannot bring himself to give up one for the other, and he gives up both. But he reserves the right to derive from each the greatest possible passive enjoyment. And this enjoyment is Irony.'[4] Professor Mudrick, writing on Jane Austen, calls irony a 'neutral

1. Sören Kierkegaard, *Kierkegaard's Concluding Unscientific Postscript*, trans. by David F. Swenson and Walter Lowrie, Princeton, 1941, p. 450.

2. Haakon M. Chevalier, *The Ironic Temper: Anatole France and His Time*, New York, 1932, p. 42. 3. ibid., p. 12. 4. ibid., p. 79.

discoverer and explorer of incongruities' and says that 'of itself it draws no conclusions'.[1] That this is an over-simplification can be seen by a further look at *Don Quixote*. Here are two world views presented and contrasted: the chivalric, as epitomized in the hero; and the common-sense, as represented by Sancho Panza. In the course of the book it becomes clear that Cervantes, though he sharply satirizes the noble philosophy of *Jerusalem Delivered*, much prefers it to the necessary, ordinary, matter-of-fact approach of Sancho Panza. This is not to say that the author abandons one for the other; there is a duality profoundly ironic. But neither is he uncommitting. Take, for instance, the famous chapter (I, xxii) in which Don Quixote (wearing a basin on his head and riding the ridiculous Rosinante) frees the galley slaves and is rewarded for his pains by both insults and a severe stoning. It seems to me that the reader of this chapter must applaud the nobility of the sentiment which prompts Don Quixote's act, and at the same time censure the hero's arrant foolishness, his inadequacy of judgement, in performing the deed. The whole relationship of Cervantes to the world view which he presents is extremely complex; but it is perfectly apparent that he does not remove himself irresponsibly from the matters which concern him so deeply; nor does he fail to make clear that Don Quixote (*because* of his noble predilections) does sometimes perform acts worthy of reproach. In short, Cervantes judges, he commits himself.

On the other hand, and as is already evident, no ironist can be doctrinaire. None of them sees a clear and present answer. There is vigour, there is humility, there is sympathy, in the ironist's search, there is judgement finally – but never serene certainty. Irony comes as the result of the quest for meaning in the universe, as the result of human experience; it is not a piece of equipment, like an entrenching tool, with which a man starts out. And this result is the divided vision – that of Chaucer, Cervantes, Swift, and Jane Austen.

1. Marvin Mudrick, *Jane Austen: Irony as Defense and Discovery*, p. 3.

The ironic man may look at the contradictions in human experience tragically or comically. Whether he does the one or the other (or perhaps both) depends upon facts and dispositions separate from, though perhaps not easily separable from, his inclination to irony. Nevertheless, there is a tendency to think that irony and humour must coexist: Saintsbury, for example, remarks that 'an ironist without humour is almost inconceivable'.[1] But Meredith has already taught us that the humorous perception is one of incongruity in man, between what he is and what he thinks he is, between expectation and fulfilment, pretence and actuality. The touchstone of the comic apprehension is a belief in common sense, a confidence that corrigibility is no dream.[2] The ironic perception, on the other hand, is, as we have seen, one of contradictions in human experience – not merely of closable gaps. This suggests that Jane Austen's novels can be read on more than one level, and it is to that level that we shall turn shortly.

Meanwhile, it may be well to point out that there may be irony without humour. Oedipus diligently searches for the slayer of King Laius, when he himself has unknowingly done the deed: the central irony of the play consists in the contrast between human justice and divine justice: it is no mere incongruity, but a flat contradiction. Axel Heyst, in *Victory*, risks personal involvement by helping a desperate Morrison, who is so grateful that he journeys to England to promote a coaling scheme in order to repay Heyst. There Morrison dies: and it is an irony (which Conrad does not omit to indicate) that the impulse lying behind this chain of circumstances should be generous and, in a sense, selfless; ironic that Heyst should have sent Morrison to destruction when the very opposite was intended. But no one laughs.

High tragedy and deep irony are often, perhaps always, closely related. The essence of the tragic vision comes in the

1. George Saintsbury, *A Saintsbury Miscellany: Selection from His Essays and Scrap Books*, New York, 1947, p. 136.

2. See George Meredith, *An Essay on Comedy and the Uses of the Comic Spirit*, London, 1898, pp. 28, 62 ff.

painful realization of the distance between divine possibility and human aspiration. Tragedy thus moves on two – or at least two – levels, the divine and the human; one of the signs of tragedy is the concern for the suprahuman, whether it be the mythological system of the Greeks, or the Christian scheme, or another. For tragedy is concerned not only with morality (in its broadest sense) but with the wellsprings of human action. Kafka's *The Castle* turns upon the exploration of the contrast, indeed the contradiction, between the human and the divine. K.'s quest is to understand, to set up lines of communications, to mediate – but he is unsuccessful. Here are tragedy and irony together.

So much, then, for irony in its subjective aspect. There is not only historical sanction for considering irony as a world view, there is historical evidence to suggest that the ironist is characterized by his recognition of the antitheses in human experience: his is an interested objectivity; he is detached but not indifferent, withdrawn but not removed. He may, as an observer of the human scene, be moved to compassion, disgust, laughter, disdain, sympathy, or horror – the whole range of reaction is evidently his: what distinguishes him uniquely is a rare and artistically fruitful combination of complexity, distance, implication.

But the artist is not the work of art: between the artistic impulse and the created object lie two transfiguring facts – the fact of the unconscious and the fact of materials. Given the artist's skill, there is not, nor can there be, a point-to-point correspondence between his conscious ratiocinations and what he creates. 'And when the process is over,' one artist tells us, 'when the picture or symphony or lyric or novel (or whatever it is) is complete, the artist, looking back on it, will wonder how on earth he did it. And indeed he did not do it on earth.' [1] This is said here by way of shifting focus to the work of art. How does the ironic artist express his vision? The question must be answered formally: we must look – in the case of the

1. E. M. Forster, 'The *Raison d'Être* of Criticism in the Arts', in *Two Cheers for Democracy*, New York, 1951, pp. 114, 115.

novel – to subject, structure, characterization, and style – those inseparables which must, for the purposes of analysis, be separated.

The ironic theme, or subject, is one of contradiction, and to discover the theme requires a whole and disinterested judgement of the novel. 'What is it about?' is at once the most important critical question and the most difficult to answer, for both totality and firmness of impression must be experienced from the work of art. So far as irony is concerned there is an additional difficulty, owing to the litotes and antiphrasis commonly called ironic, but which may in fact not underlie a thematic irony. A good example of the un-ironic is provided by *Jonathan Wild the Great*, the subject of which is human villainy. Here Fielding draws a contrast between the dynamic, unscrupulous, 'great' hero and the generous, naïve, 'silly' Heartfree. But this is not an ironic work, despite the author's free use of rhetorical irony (about which more will be said later). For here is contrast merely, not contradiction: Fielding's commitment is wholly to the values of Heartfree; they are exposed, and strengthened, in the conflict with Jonathan Wild.

But in *Billy Budd* there is genuine irony. Billy is 'a sort of upright barbarian, much such perhaps as Adam might presumably have been ere the urbane Serpent wriggled himself into his company'. He is simple, honest, direct, candid; and it is a combination of his noble qualities (together with the stutter that makes him momentarily dumb) that causes him to strike the complicated and disingenuous Master-at-Arms, John Claggart. ' "Struck dead by an angel of God. Yet the angel must hang!" ' – so exclaims Captain Vere, thus expressing the central irony of the story. For Billy strikes Claggart in righteous anger, 'a generous young heart's virgin experience of the diabolical incarnate and effective in some men ...'.[1] It is cruel, but just and necessary in worldly terms, that Billy should hang. But the story displays, with painful clarity, the

1. Herman Melville, *Billy Budd*, ed. F. Barron Freeman, London, 1948, pp. 147, 229, 259.

unresolvable conflicts between justice and mercy, experience and innocence, noble anger and devilish calculation.

What is required in many instances is a fresh look at novels whose themes have been too shallowly interpreted. And here we can get back to Jane Austen. As we have already seen, the theme of *Sense and Sensibility* is stated in the title, and throughout much of the book Sensibility appears to be the straw-man which Sense is to, and does in fact, overthrow: Marianne makes a prudent marriage. Yet Sense is not the only victor: for by a parallel irony Elinor marries, for love, a man whose early history discloses him to be energetic, passionate, sensitive. It is on the level of irony that the depth of the book becomes evident. There is, it seems to me, an irreconcilable contradiction set up between the two modes; and, so far as the intention of the novel is concerned (it may not, however, have been Jane Austen's fully conscious intention), there is disclosed a profound ambivalence. What the book most significantly illustrates is that both Sense and Sensibility are desirable, indeed necessary, for a whole life: but they are mutually exclusive. Thus the novel goes beyond the boundaries of satire, it exceeds the requirements of pure comedy, and becomes ironic: the not insubstantial theme of the book is that the claims of Sense and Sensibility are irreconcilable.

In support of this view, I shall cite a good deal of evidence in subsequent chapters. Meanwhile, it may not be amiss to sketch my reasons for thinking that the book is more than a mere didactic treatise in which Sense triumphs and Sensibility is depressed. In the first place, there is the undeniable attractiveness of Marianne, of whose 'burning human heart' George Moore speaks with approbation.[1] We laugh at her follies – at her doctrine of 'first attachments', at her Cowperesque apostrophes to Norland, at her enthusiasm for accepting the gift of a horse named (not unsignificantly) 'Queen Mab': but we sympathize with her miseries – when she is thrown over so summarily by Willoughby, when she has to endure his grossly insulting letter, and in her efforts after she has been 'awakened

1. Quoted in R. W. Chapman, *Jane Austen Facts and Problems*, p. 193.

to a *reasonable* exertion ...'.[1] There is the incontravertible fact of her marriage to Colonel Brandon, which certainly represents an alteration from her first youthful enthusiasm. On the other hand, if she is meant merely to exemplify an unlaudable predisposition to 'enthusiasm', why is she so lovable? Why, indeed, is she not portrayed as an Isabella Thorpe? And why is John Willoughby's abandonment of her effected so brutally? – for certainly any credulous young girl might be taken in by him. The answers to these questions must be that in valuing Marianne Dashwood, Jane Austen values sensibility, however limited she may feel this quality to be. Again, *Sense and Sensibility* has no single heroine (as *Pride and Prejudice*, for all its approbation of Jane Bennet, does): Elinor and Marianne are accorded equal status as heroines; indeed, the arrangement of the story draws very obvious parallels between the two girls: Elinor's *andante* attachment to Edward Ferrars, Marianne's *allegrissimo* adventure with Willoughby – each of the sisters disappointed in her hopes, each taking her disappointment in a different way; both, at last, finding husbands who are suitable for them. It is this duality in the book which gives it substance and depth, however unsatisfactory it may be structurally.

Even *Northanger Abbey* goes beyond the burlesque, to a tender and perceptive exploration of the boundaries of good sense. Basically, Catherine Morland is sensible; her only areas of illusionment are those which the novel of terror might involve her in. Thus she becomes a good friend of Isabella Thorpe because in the Gothic convention a confidante is indispensable, but John Thorpe is too ridiculously boorish ever to be a Gothic hero – Catherine dislikes him almost on sight. And she is not long in seeing through even Isabella's shallowness, nor does she hesitate to like Eleanor Tilney for 'her good sense and good breeding'. But the novel takes on a dimension beyond that of common sense: for that attribute will not allow Catherine to deal adequately with her summary dismissal from Northanger Abbey; it will not enable her to

1. *Sense and Sensibility*, p. 342 (italics my own).

console herself completely, when she can no longer expect to marry Henry Tilney. Back home, she finds that 'there are some situations of the human mind in which good sense has very little power ...'.[1] So, starting as a burlesque, *Northanger Abbey* ends as a critique not only of the vapidly sentimental Gothic novel, but also of common sense, which Jane Austen so highly regards, but whose limitations she is not afraid to set forth.

Sense and Sensibility is a study of opposites; *Pride and Prejudice* is not: it is much more complex; for, as one examines the book, one is struck with the fact that Pride leads to Prejudice and Prejudice invites Pride; and that both have their corresponding virtues bound up within them. Indeed, a key to the ironic significance of the book lies in the following conversation between Elizabeth and Bingley:

'Whatever I do is done in a hurry ... [he says] and therefore if I should resolve to quit Netherfield, I should probably be off in five minutes. At present, however, I consider myself as quite fixed here.'

'That is exactly what I should have supposed of you,' said Elizabeth.

'You begin to comprehend me, do you?' cried he, turning towards her.

'Oh! yes – I understand you perfectly.'

'I wish I might take this for a compliment; but to be so easily seen through I am afraid is pitiful.'

'That is as it happens. It does not necessarily follow that a deep, intricate character is more or less estimable than such a one as yours.'

'Lizzy,' cried her mother, 'remember where you are, and do not run on in the wild manner that you are suffered to do at home.'

'I did not know before,' continued Bingley immediately, 'that you were a studier of character. It must be an amusing study.'

'Yes, but intricate characters are the *most* amusing. They have at least that advantage.'[2]

1. *Northanger Abbey*, p. 239. 2. *Pride and Prejudice*, p. 42.

Elizabeth puts it light-heartedly; but on the ironic level *Pride and Prejudice* concerns itself with Intricacy and Simplicity as those terms apply to personality. Each has its virtues and each its defects: they are contradictory, and the supreme irony is that Intricacy, which is so much deeper, carries with it grave dangers unknown to Simplicity.

We have already had a look at Elizabeth and Darcy, and Jane and Bingley. But there is a third pair, Charlotte and Wickham, who are the focus of this deeper meaning: they are a comment on Elizabeth and Darcy, whose breadth and depth involve them in the dangers of Prejudice and Pride. If the central couple is flanked on the one side by the unexceptionable Bingley and Jane, it is flanked on the other by Charlotte and Wickham, both of whom have a great deal of the cleverness of the two main characters, but whose concern for worldly success undermines their virtue. *Pride and Prejudice* is thus concerned with the contradictions of human personality – one might say, the price of intelligence.

Beyond the consideration of Emma's conceit is what seems to me the major theme of Jane Austen's greatest novel: 'tenderness of heart'. In a moment of self-awareness – it is a main climax of the book – Emma reflects:

> 'There is no charm equal to tenderness of heart,' said she ... to herself. 'There is nothing to be compared to it. Warmth and tenderness of heart, with an affectionate, open manner, will beat all the clearness of head in the world, for attraction. I am sure it will. It is tenderness of heart which makes my dear father so generally beloved – which gives Isabella all her popularity. – I have it not – but I know how to prize and respect it. – Harriet is my superior in all the charm and all the felicity it gives. Dear Harriet! – I would not change you for the clearest-headed, longest-sighted, best-judging female breathing.' [1]

This is the other side of the coin. Emma's tendency to self-importance, her confidence in her own infallibility, her wish to run things – these are the reparable defects which constitute

1. *Emma*, p. 269.

the comic stuff of the novel. But the tenderness of heart which in fact Emma possesses in abundance is often obscured, conquered, or deflected: the irony of *Emma* is that tenderness of heart opposes itself to sharpness and clarity of perception.

Consider Harriet, Emma's brainless little companion, who is so sweet, so tender, and so completely lacking in any kind of judgement that she is as malleable as putty; consider Mr Woodhouse and Isabella, who are both unfailingly tender also, and equally unperceptive – none of these characters can command the admiration (except as artistic creations) which we accord Emma. On the other hand, Frank Churchill is, though very clever, notably wanting in the tenderness which the others have. Emma comes straight up against the ironic problem, and declares herself on the side of tenderness at the expense of other qualities. The problem remains nevertheless, for her as well as the others.

And although Overpersuasion is, in one aspect, the theme of *Persuasion*, the story is also one of the conflict between parental authority (prudence) on the one hand, and the sanguine hopes for love, on the other. Which is right? Which should be obeyed? At first glance it would seem that the book underscores the value of yielding to the importunities of love, regardless. Anne has – before the happy ending – more than one bitter moment of self-reproach because she attended too well the advice of her elders; only a series of coincidences makes possible her reunion with Frederick Wentworth. Yet we find her saying, near the end, ' "I was right in submitting to" ' Lady Russell.[1] Prudence and love are thus in conflict, as indeed they are in *Pride and Prejudice*, when Charlotte makes her purely prudential match with William Collins. Here, as in the earlier novel, both qualities are seen to be desirable, both are defended with warm sympathy by Jane Austen; but neither can be achieved without some sacrifice of the other. Anne Elliot and Frederick Wentworth do come together happily at the end of *Persuasion*, but only after almost a decade of being apart.

1. *Persuasion*, p. 246.

But we are already at the point of analysing structure. How does Jane Austen tell her story? The question can be answered by reference to her techniques of point of view. And it is to a consideration of this aspect of her novels that we shall turn in the following chapter.

CHAPTER II

Narrative Management: Points of View

IN relation to her novels Jane Austen stands sometimes coolly apart – as apparently (and just as pretendingly) objective as the Chaucer of the *Troilus*; at the opposite extreme, she sets herself down, *in propria persona*, in the centre of her works with quite as much self-consciousness as the Thackeray of *Vanity Fair*. She is by turns omniscient and ignorant, humble and sententious, direct and oblique, the dramatist and the teller of tales. Unshackled by more modern theories, her point of view varies; it is sly, often intentionally misleading – or at least very delicately subtle: quite unobtrusive transitions carry the reader from one viewpoint to another, and only the closest attention will enable him to ferret out the real intention of the passage in question. So point of view as one of the wellsprings of Jane Austen's meaning demands inquiry.

In the drama the very nature of the medium permits an exterior viewpoint whence irony can proceed, or rather through which it exists: 'dramatic irony' is always, and rightly, defined in terms of viewpoint.[1] But in narratives meant to be read, several methods, including that of dramatic irony, are employed. Professor Elliott has recently shown that *A Tale of a Tub* achieves its unity through a subtle and complex point of view: the purported writer of the work is not Swift but 'his favourite ingénu, an "I" who egregiously identifies him-

1. G. G. Sedgewick's study, *Of Irony, Especially in Drama*, University of Toronto, Philology and Literature Series, No. 10 (1935), is invaluable on this subject.

self with the very abuses that Swift is attacking'.[1] Nor have many critics failed to notice that Conrad's management of point of view yields up complex ironies: in *Lord Jim*, for instance, the hero never once speaks directly; the writer is ostensibly relating a story told by Marlow who has pieced the tale together from accounts not only by Jim but by several others.

In Jane Austen's novels there are six characteristic points of view – separable and susceptible of analysis. All of them are well-recognized novelistic techniques; none is necessarily ironic – though some, for reasons which will be set forth below, are sharper than others as ironic instruments. Needless to say, any effort to set up categories must fail of complete success: Jane Austen is richer than a categorical examination can allow; and to separate is to do violence both to the unity of each novel and to the contextual harmony of the passages examined. Yet having made these obvious qualifications, one can see the value of such an approach; the result is so illuminating; it clears a hundred ambiguities and misapprehensions; it makes plainer the intention. Without, then, examining every page of every one of the novels, let us turn to some leading examples of each kind of viewpoint from which our author tells her stories.

I. THE 'OBJECTIVE' ACCOUNT

Sometimes Jane Austen poses as an historian, in possession of all the facts, interested only in presenting them as they have happened and interpreting them only as they themselves force evaluation from their very sum; at other times, she poses as a neutral observer, as the silent member amongst those present, recording facts and disinterested impressions from what she is witnessing. That is, she sometimes seems a chronicler of the

1. Robert C. Elliott, 'Swift's *Tale of a Tub*: an Essay in Problems of Structure', *Publications of the Modern Language Association of America*, LXVI (1951), p. 443.

past, and at others a narrator of the present. But neutrality is, in fact, quite impossible for Jane Austen; she will not let the facts speak for themselves, for she does not believe that facts can be articulate.

When Mr John Dashwood pays a belated call on Mrs Jennings in Berkeley Street, the event is reported as follows:

> His visit was duly paid. He came with a pretence at an apology from their [Elinor's and Marianne's] sister-in-law, for not coming too; 'but she was so much engaged with her mother, that really she had no leisure for going any where'. Mrs Jennings, however, assured him directly, that she should not stand upon ceremony, for they were all cousins, or something like it, and she should certainly wait on Mrs John Dashwood very soon, and bring her sisters to see her. His manners to *them*, though calm, were perfectly kind; to Mrs Jennings most attentively civil; and on Colonel Brandon's coming in soon after himself, he eyed him with a curiosity which seemed to say, that he only wanted to know him to be rich, to be equally civil to *him*.[1]

From this passage alone the reader is able to understand a good deal about John Dashwood and about Mrs Jennings: the former's civility and its limits, the latter's insensitivity to the most transparent kind of excuse and her boundless good-heartedness. It is in the arrangement of this account that the unobjective intention discloses itself: the thin ground of John Dashwood's civility is exposed only at the end of the paragraph, and the reader is forced to think back on what has gone before. Doubtless he *is* civil, but partly through an impurity of motive.

Catherine Morland is introduced to us with apparent straightforwardness:

> No one who had ever seen Catherine Morland in her infancy, would have supposed her born to be an heroine. Her situation in life, the character of her father and mother, her own person and disposition, were all equally against her. Her father was a clergyman, without being neglected, or poor, and a very respectable man, though his name was Richard – and he had never been hand-

1. *Sense and Sensibility*, pp. 222, 223.

some. He had a considerable independence, besides two good livings – and he was not in the least addicted to locking up his daughters. Her mother was a woman of useful plain sense, with a good temper, and, what is more remarkable, with a good constitution. She had three sons before Catherine was born; and instead of dying in bringing the latter into the world, as any body might expect, she still lived on – lived to have six children more – to see them growing up around her, and to enjoy excellent health herself.[1]

Who is speaking here? Who is telling the story? Obviously, Jane Austen is identifying herself with a sentimental novelist. She might, for instance, be identifying herself with Goldsmith in describing Catherine Morland's father – and drawing a satiric comparison between Charles Primrose and Richard Morland. And who would expect Mrs Morland to die in giving birth to the heroine? Only the reader of the sentimental novel. Thus there is a double pretence here, the pretence that the author is another in the long line of sentimental novelists, and the calculated illusion that the audience will be composed of readers of this genre. Certainly Jane Austen is more transparent here than elsewhere in her novels, and the reason is plain: *Northanger Abbey* is more nearly tied to parody or burlesque, where simple reversals obtain.

Yet she is not by any means consistent in this pose:

Miss Tilney had a good figure, a pretty face, and a very agreeable countenance; and her air, though it had not all the decided pretension, the resolute stilishness of Miss Thorpe's, had more real elegance. Her manners shewed good sense and good breeding; they were neither shy, nor affectedly open; and she seemed capable of being young, attractive, and at a ball, without wanting to fix the attention of every man near her, and without exaggerated feelings of extatic delight or inconceivable vexation on every little trifling occurrence.[2]

Clearly a different person is telling the story in this passage – one who sees right through Isabella Thorpe, and quite fully recognizes the limitations of this sentimental confidante. Here

1. *Northanger Abbey*, p. 13.
2. *Northanger Abbey*, pp. 55, 56.

is the truth as Jane Austen sees it. But she leaves it to the reader to discriminate between the two narrators of this story.

After the delicious dialogue of the first chapter of *Pride and Prejudice* the author sums up the characters of Mr and Mrs Bennet:

> Mr Bennet was so odd a mixture of quick parts, sarcastic humour, reserve, and caprice, that the experience of three and twenty years had been insufficient to make his wife understand his character. *Her* mind was less difficult to develope. She was a woman of mean understanding, little information, and uncertain temper. When she was discontented she fancied herself nervous. The business of her life was to get her daughters married; its solace was visiting and news.[1]

Here, in very economical compass, is an accurate sketch of both characters, drawn by someone who has a complete insight into them. Yet the chapter has begun with some grandiloquent statements as to the marriageability of rich young men; statements which cannot represent the author's opinion. Actually, the reader can at this point only guess that Mr and Mrs Bennet are being truly described, but the guess can be grounded on the conversation which they have just completed. And notice what Jane Austen withholds: she does not tell us of Mr Bennet's wanton irresponsibility nor of Mrs Bennet's malevolent selfishness; the author simply states some conditions from which these can follow.

Of the relationship between Darcy and Bingley the reader gets an analytical account:

> Bingley was endeared to Darcy by the easiness, openness, ductility of his temper, though no disposition could offer a greater contrast to his own, and though with his own he never appeared dissatisfied. On the strength of Darcy's regard Bingley had the firmest reliance, and of his judgement the highest opinion. In understanding Darcy was the superior. Bingley was by no means deficient, but Darcy was clever.[2]

1. *Pride and Prejudice*, p. 5. 2. ibid., p. 16.

Again Jane Austen omnisciently presents insights into her characters; and, as there is no suggestion in any of her language or syntax that she is not being altogether straightforward, we accept this statement at its face value. On the other hand, in recording Mr Bennet's early history, the author, while apparently giving an objective account, actually shifts rapidly from one point of view to another:

Had Elizabeth's opinion been all drawn from her own family, she could not have formed a very pleasing picture of conjugal felicity or domestic comfort. Her father, captivated by youth and beauty, and that appearance of good humour, which youth and beauty generally give, had married a woman whose weak understanding and illiberal mind, had very early in their marriage put an end to all real affection for her. Respect, esteem, and confidence, had vanished for ever; and all his views of domestic happiness were overthrown. But Mr Bennet was not of a disposition to seek comfort for the disappointment which his own imprudence had brought on, in any of those pleasures which too often console the unfortunate for their folly or their vices. He was fond of the country and of books; and from these tastes had arisen his principal enjoyments. To his wife he was very little otherwise indebted, than as her ignorance and folly had contributed to his amusement. This is not the sort of happiness which a man would in general wish to owe to his wife; but where other powers of entertainment are wanting, the true philosopher will derive benefit from such as are given.[1]

The mention of Elizabeth in the first sentence suggests that the author is preparing to present the heroine's impressions of her father; this is the case: in the following paragraph, the viewpoint is that of Elizabeth. But here Jane Austen relates certain facts of which Elizabeth cannot have such direct knowledge; in fact, the author is speaking, and she even introduces several sententious phrases: '... that appearance of good humour which youth and beauty generally give' must be admitted as an objective truth if we are to accept the fact that an intelligent man would marry a silly woman; 'those

1. ibid., p. 236.

pleasures which too often console the unfortunate for their folly or their vices' is stated with such moderation and straightforwardness that we must believe it; but the last sentence must be immediately suspect if we reflect on Jane Austen's diction: the ambiguous word 'entertainment', which in the eighteenth century meant both 'support, sustenance', and 'that which affords interest or amusement' (*N.E.D.*); and her mention of 'the true philosopher', the slightly grand epithet for something much more ordinary – a characteristic method of achieving an ironic purpose.

Jane Austen describes Fanny Price on her arrival at Mansfield Park:

> Fanny Price was at this time just ten years old, and though there might not be much in her first appearance to captivate, there was, at least, nothing to disgust her relations. She was small of her age, with no glow of complexion, nor any other striking beauty; exceedingly timid and shy, and shrinking from notice; but her air, though awkward, was not vulgar, her voice was sweet, and when she spoke, her countenance was pretty. Sir Thomas and Lady Bertram received her very kindly, and Sir Thomas, seeing how much she needed encouragement, tried to be all that was conciliating; but he had to work against a most untoward gravity of deportment – and Lady Bertram, without taking half so much trouble, or speaking one word where he spoke ten, by the mere aid of a good-humoured smile, became immediately the less awful character of the two.[1]

At first, the texture of this paragraph suggests that the author may be the neutral observer, sitting in the corner of the parlour at Mansfield Park, and remarking little Fanny Price as she makes her first appearance before her aunt and uncle. Everything related could be observed or easily guessed at by an intelligent onlooker – everything but what is described in the last few words, for there Jane Austen takes us directly into Fanny's mind to show her reaction to the meeting.

When, after Mr Norris's death, the Grants come to Mansfield Parsonage, Jane Austen introduces them as follows:

1. *Mansfield Park*, p. 12.

The Grants, showing a disposition to be friendly and sociable, gave great satisfaction in the main among their new acquaintance. They had their faults, and Mrs Norris soon found them out. The Dr was very fond of eating, and would have a good dinner every day; and Mrs Grant, instead of contriving to gratify him at little expense, gave her cook as high wages as they did at Mansfield Park, and was scarcely ever seen in her offices. Mrs Norris could not speak with any temper of such grievances, nor of the quantity of butter and eggs that were regularly consumed in the house.[1]

Because the first sentence is apparently an accurate statement as to the Grants' impression on the people of the neighbourhood, we accept it as objective and proceed to the second, where our suspicions are aroused by the mention of Mrs Norris, whose reactions we have already learned to distrust. If the Grants have faults, does Mrs Norris know what they are? Obviously the list set forth here only reflects her own prejudices – as the word 'grievances' afterwards suggests. Thus Jane Austen has slyly shifted her point of view from herself to one of her most unpleasant characters.

After intimately recording Fanny's refusal of Henry Crawford's proposal of marriage, Jane Austen stands off from her heroine and tells us:

Fanny knew her own meaning, but was no judge of her own manner. Her manner was incurably gentle, and she was not aware how much it concealed the sternness of her purpose. Her diffidence, gratitude, and softness, made every expression of indifference seem almost an effort of self-denial; seem at least, to be giving nearly as much pain to herself as to him.[2]

Jane Austen is speaking in this passage; apparently she feels the reader will not comprehend Henry Crawford's persistence, if this point is not made.

At the beginning of *Emma*, the author rapidly sketches in the background of the heroine, but in the fourth paragraph:

The real evils indeed of Emma's situation were the power of having rather too much of her own way, and a disposition to think

1. ibid., p. 31. 2. ibid., p. 327.

a little too well of herself; these were the disadvantages which threatened alloy to her many enjoyments. The danger, however, was at present so unperceived, that they did not by any means rank as misfortunes with her.[1]

The chronicler has stopped, and the reflective moralist takes over. Jane Austen would have us know at once what the theme of the book will be; she tells us in the midst of a recital of facts, so quietly that we may overlook this direct intervention on the part of the author.

Harriet Smith's encounter with gypsies, and her rescue by Frank Churchill, are of supreme importance in *Emma*; on this incident much of the irony of the book depends: Emma will for a dangerously long time believe Harriet's allusions to her rescuer to refer to Frank Churchill, while in fact the girl is alluding to Mr Knightley's gallantry in dancing with her. So Jane Austen does not trust her to describe what happens on her walk along Richmond road; and there is another good reason for this: that Harriet is such a poor observer.

A [gypsy] child on the watch, came towards them to beg; and Miss Bickerton, excessively frightened, gave a great scream, and calling on Harriet to follow her, ran up a steep bank, cleared a slight hedge at the top, and made the best of her way by a short cut back to Highbury. But poor Harriet could not follow.[2]

So, with clarity and objectivity does the author record the entire incident; the reader cannot afterwards misinterpret it – nor can Emma, whose misconstruction arises partly from the close conjunction of rescues, partly from her desire to make a match between Harriet and Frank, partly from her blindness in not even considering Mr Knightley as one of the candidates for Harriet's hand.

And the author rings down the curtain of this novel with a final (and delightful) ironic touch. Here is the marriage ceremony of Mr Knightley and Emma:

The wedding was very much like other weddings, where the parties have no taste for finery or parade; and Mrs Elton, from

1. *Emma*, pp. 5, 6. 2. ibid., p. 333.

the particulars detailed by her husband, thought it all extremely shabby, and very inferior to her own. – 'Very little white satin, very few lace veils; a most pitiful business! – Selina would stare when she heard of it.' – But, in spite of these deficiencies, the wishes, the hopes, the confidence, the predictions of the small band of true friends who witnessed the ceremony, were fully answered in the perfect happiness of the union.[1]

The identification of Jane Austen with Mrs Elton (in the phrase, 'in spite of these deficiencies') is a thoroughly characteristic touch – transparent when we reflect that the vicar's wife has not been invited to the wedding, while 'the true friends' are present.

The chronicler of *Persuasion* lets us know in the first paragraph the sum and substance of Sir Walter Elliot's character:

Sir Walter Elliot, of Kellynch-hall, in Somersetshire, was a man who, for his own amusement, never took up any book but the Baronetage; there he found occupation for an idle hour, and consolation in a distressed one; there his faculties were roused into admiration and respect, by contemplating the limited remnant of the earliest patents; there any unwelcome sensations, arising from domestic affairs, changed naturally into pity and contempt, as he turned over the almost endless creations of the last century – and there, if every other leaf were powerless, he could read his own history with an interest which never failed – this was the page at which the favourite volume always opened:

ELLIOT OF KELLYNCH-HALL...[2]

The reader's impression of Sir Walter is immediately that the baronet is ironically perceived by the author. There are several reasons: the double-negative of the first relative clause; the grand Johnsonian balance of phrase and clause; the periodicity of the fourth main clause; the anti-climax of the whole complicated sentence. Orotundity of diction and syntax, to be contrasted with the commonplace fact that Sir Walter is an egregious snob, are what give this magnificent introduction its sharpness, through which (or beyond which) the reader sees a far from neutral chronicler.

1. ibid., p. 484. 2. *Persuasion*, p. 3.

Richard Musgrove's early demise is a source of grief to his parents – after Captain Wentworth comes to Kellynch, and they learn that their son served under the newcomer. Wentworth has too nice a regard for the bereaved parents to tell us about their son, so Jane Austen discloses the facts of the situation.

> The real circumstances of this pathetic piece of family history were that the Musgroves had had the ill fortune of a very troublesome, hopeless son; and the good fortune to lose him before he reached his twentieth year; that he had been sent to sea, because he was stupid and unmanageable on shore; that he had been very little cared for at any time by his family, though quite as much as he deserved; seldom heard of, and scarcely at all regretted, when the intelligence of his death abroad had worked its way to Uppercross, two years before.[1]

The omniscient narrator of the story has stepped in, not only to record some facts which we could not otherwise know, but also to make some very sharp judgements lest the reader be confused by the grief of the Musgroves and the diplomacy of Captain Wentworth. By himself, Richard Musgrove is unimportant – he never once appears in the novel, alive – but his memory has its place by way of a comment on the living characters in the story.

The dramatist always faces the problem of passing over action which is necessary to the development of his piece, but which for one reason or another – for instance, the impossibility of staging it, or the fact that it reiterates what has already been made clear – must be omitted from the action actually represented. The novelist is not thus limited; he can summarize. And summary is, for several reasons, necessary: to avoid the repetition of what has already been related at some length; to abbreviate what would otherwise be a tedious and unnecessary dialogue; to achieve a distance from which the reader can see more clearly the significance of certain

1. *Persuasion*, pp. 50, 51.

incidents; and (from a purely technical standpoint) to avoid the inaccuracy of reporting on an area of human intercourse with which the author is not familiar.

When Edward Ferrars comes to visit the Dashwoods at Barton College, he is so diffident, so hesitant, so inarticulate, so cool, that Elinor cannot help contrasting this behaviour to that of the Edward she knew at Norland. But this is all made clear almost at once – so that the author, in one short paragraph, summarizes his visit:

> Edward remained a week at the cottage; he was earnestly pressed by Mrs Dashwood to stay longer; but as if he were bent only on self-mortification, he seemed resolved to be gone when his enjoyment among his friends was at the height. His spirits, during the last two or three days, though still very unequal, were greatly improved – he grew more and more partial to the house and environs – never spoke of going away without a sigh – declared his time to be wholly disengaged – even doubted to what place he should go when he left them – but still, go he must. Never had any week passed so quickly – he could hardly believe it to be gone. He said so repeatedly; other things he said too, which marked the turn of his feelings and gave the lie to his actions. He had no pleasure at Norland; he detested being in town; but either to Norland or London, he must go. He valued their kindness beyond any thing, and his greatest happiness was in being with them. Yet he must leave them at the end of a week, in spite of their wishes and his own, and without any restraint on his time.[1]

The objectivity of this recital is broken by the subordinate clause, 'as if he were bent only on self-mortification', which is a thought not likely to occur to Mrs Dashwood but must be a reaction of the narrator. Yet Jane Austen keeps herself well withdrawn here – even suggesting conversation between Edward and his hostess.

After Lucy Steele has convinced Elinor Dashwood that she has been engaged to Edward for four years, the latter does not see him for some time. At last they meet:

1. *Sense and Sensibility*, p. 101.

> [Elinor] forced herself, after a moment's recollection, to welcome him, with a look and manner that were almost easy, and almost open; and another struggle, another effort still improved them. She would not allow the presence of Lucy, nor the consciousness of some injustice towards herself, to deter her from saying that she was happy to see him, and that she had very much regretted being from home, when he called before in Berkeley-street.[1]

There are two obvious advantages to this summary: in the first place, the reader is spared a dialogue which could hardly be interesting; in the second, the author presents this paragraph from Elinor's viewpoint, so that the heroine's reaction can be detailed in all its ramifications.

While Marianne is ill at Cleveland, with her 'hectic symptoms', Willoughby appears unexpectedly and has a lengthy interview with Elinor, during which he explains away as much as possible his own beastly conduct towards Marianne. He is humble, he is penitent, he is long-winded; but Elinor must report the sense of this conversation to her sister. This she does, but the reader is not forced to listen to it again.

> She managed the recital, as she hoped, with address; prepared her anxious listener with caution; related simply and honestly the chief points on which Willoughby grounded his apology; did justice to his repentance, and softened only his protestations of present regard. Marianne said not a word. – She trembled, her eyes were fixed on the ground, and her lips became whiter than even sickness had left them. A thousand inquiries sprung up from her heart, but she dared not urge one.[2]

There are actually three points of view in this paragraph: Elinor's at the beginning; the 'objective' narrator's in the middle (in the remark that Miss Dashwood 'did justice to his repentance'); and Marianne's at the end.

In *Northanger Abbey* Jane Austen pretendingly identifies herself, so far as possible, with the Gothic novelist and leaves

1. *Sense and Sensibility*, p. 241. Compare a summary for the same purposes, pp. 283, 284.
2. ibid., pp. 347, 348.

it to the reader to make the ironic reversals necessary to understand the real viewpoint from which the story is being told. This fact is as clear in the accounts of action as in the recital of the histories of her characters. The final preparations for Catherine's departure from home and the journey to Bath are summarized thus:

> It is remarkable ... that she [Sarah, Catherine's sister] neither insisted on Catherine's writing by every post, nor exacted her promise of transmitting the character of every new acquaintance, nor a detail of every interesting conversation that Bath might produce. Every thing indeed relative to this important journey was done, on the part of the Morlands, with a degree of moderation and composure, which seemed rather consistent with the common feelings of common life, than with the refined susceptibilities, the tender emotions which the first separation of a heroine from her family ought always to excite. ...
>
> Under these unpromising auspices, the parting took place, and the journey began. It was performed with suitable quietness and uneventful safety. Neither robbers nor tempests befriended them, nor one lucky overturn to introduce them to the hero. Nothing more alarming occurred than a fear on Mrs Allen's side, of having once left her clogs behind her at an inn, and that fortunately proved to be groundless.[1]

Who is the narrator here, who is saying that it is 'remarkable' that Catherine's sister does not exact a number of promises from her? It is obviously a feigned narrator who relates the story – as for instance the word 'tempests' suggests, when after all a short journey from Wiltshire to Somerset is being described; or the fact that Mrs Allen's definitely unromantic wooden-soled shoes are mentioned as the only incipient adventure.

Occasionally, Jane Austen summarizes an incident or series of incidents in such a way as to disclose certain reactions which could be known only to the omniscient narrator. After William Collins's proposal to Charlotte Lucas, this paragraph occurs:

1. *Northanger Abbey*, p. 19.

Sir William and Lady Lucas were speedily applied to for their consent; and it was bestowed with a most joyful alacrity. Mr Collins's present circumstances made it a most eligible match for their daughter, to whom they could give little fortune; and his prospects of future wealth were exceedingly fair. Lady Lucas began directly to calculate with more interest than the matter had ever excited before, how many years longer Mr Bennet was likely to live; and Sir William gave it as his decided opinion, that whenever Mr Collins should be in possession of the Longbourn estate, it would be highly expedient that both he and his wife should make their appearance at St James's. The whole family in short were properly overjoyed on the occasion. The younger girls formed hopes of *coming out* a year or two sooner than they might otherwise have done; and the boys were relieved from their apprehension of Charlotte's dying an old maid.[1]

This pretends to be an objective narrative by an omniscient scribe; objectively, it is 'a most eligible match'; objectively, 'the whole family were properly overjoyed'; and the girls speak of '*coming out*'. Actually, the surrounding circumstances make it quite clear that the author has identified herself with the viewpoint of the Lucases, while maintaining the pose of narrator – and this in order to achieve the purpose of mocking the pretensions of this trades-family.

After Darcy's departure from the neighbourhood of Longbourn, Wickham freely tells the story of the former's wrongdoings to him – a story which previously he revealed only to Elizabeth.

The whole of what Elizabeth had already heard, his claims on Mr Darcy, and all that he had suffered from him, was now openly acknowledged and publicly canvassed; and every body was pleased to think how much they had always disliked Mr Darcy before they had known any thing of the matter.[2]

In the first part of this paragraph Jane Austen identifies herself with Wickham's viewpoint, in that – rather than speaking of an allegation or even one version of a story – she uses

1. *Pride and Prejudice*, p. 122. 2. ibid., p. 138.

the word 'acknowledged'. Yet this acknowledgement is rendered suspect by the hint which she then gives of the people of the neighbourhood: 'everybody was pleased to think' contains an ambiguity in the leading verb; they could either be taking pleasure in the thought, or they could *choose* to recollect what they do. Both meanings existed then, as now.

On their return to Longbourn after being married, Lydia and Wickham are described with partial objectivity; their actual words of greeting are not heard.

> Their reception from Mr Bennet, to whom they then turned [after greeting Mrs Bennet], was not quite so cordial. His countenance rather gained in austerity; and he scarcely opened his lips. The easy assurance of the young couple, indeed, was enough to provoke him. Elizabeth was disgusted, and even Miss Bennet was shocked. Lydia was Lydia still; untamed, unabashed, wild, noisy, and fearless. She turned from sister to sister, demanding their congratulations, and when at length they all sat down, looked eagerly round the room, took notice of some little alteration in it, and observed, with a laugh, that it was a great while since she had been there.[1]

The beginning and the ending of this paragraph contain what might be observed by a perceptive and evaluating witness. But the author does also take us directly into the minds of Elizabeth and Jane. Who, then, describes Lydia with the five devastating adjectives? The reader might attribute the thought to either of the Miss Bennets; but upon reflection one realizes that Jane Bennet would never censure so wholly – and in fact the adjectives have such a literary tone that they probably emanate from the narrator rather than from the mind of Elizabeth. There is at least a question as to what viewpoint is used in the sentence.

When the Miss Bertrams get acquainted with little Fanny Price, they react vigorously.

> They could not but hold her cheap on finding that she had but two sashes, and had never learnt French; and when they perceived

1. ibid., p. 315.

her to be little struck with the duet they were so good as to play, they could do no more than make her a generous present of some of their least valued toys, and leave her to herself, while they adjourned to whatever might be the favourite holiday sport of the moment, making artificial flowers or wasting gold paper.[1]

Besides saving the reader the tedium of viewing at length this rather unhappy (and no doubt not very interesting) series of incidents, Jane Austen shows us the thoughts of the two Miss Bertrams, and even pretends to share their aversions to Fanny's inadequacies; but the author then gives herself – and the two sisters – away, by the word 'wasting', which intentionally casts doubt on the validity of the Miss Bertrams' reflections.

When Henry Crawford tells his sister about his love for Fanny Price, most of the recital is reported by the author rather than quoted directly.

... he had in fact nothing to relate but his own sensations, nothing to dwell on but Fanny's charms. – Fanny's beauty of face and figure, Fanny's graces of manner and goodness of heart were the exhaustless theme. The gentleness, modesty, and sweetness of her character were warmly expatiated on, that sweetness which makes so essential a part of every woman's worth in the judgement of man, that though he sometimes loves where it is not, he can never believe it absent. Her temper he had good reason to depend on and to praise. ... Nor was this all. Henry Crawford had too much sense not to feel the worth of good principles in a wife, though he was too little accustomed to serious reflection to know them by their proper name; but when he talked of her having such a steadiness and regularity of conduct, such a high notion of honour, and such an observance of decorum as might warrant any man in the fullest dependence on her faith and integrity, he expressed what was inspired by the knowledge of her being well principled and religious.[2]

At the beginning of this passage, the author (while seeming merely to state a fact) is speaking with an understatement which is meant to contrast with the extravagant claims which Henry Crawford himself makes for Fanny. Perhaps this is

1. *Mansfield Park*, p. 14. 2. ibid., p. 294.

done to cast ridicule upon his own reversal of position – from the man who will make Fanny love him because he is bored, to the ardent lover. Yet Jane Austen feels constrained to underline the fact that this affection is serious, by telling us that he has 'too much sense not to feel the worth of good principles in a wife . . .'

While Emma and Harriet Smith are shopping at Highbury, Emma becomes bored while her friend is 'hanging over muslins and changing her mind', and so she goes to the door and watches what is going on in the street.

> Much could not be hoped from the traffic of even the busiest part of Highbury; – Mr Perry walking hastily by, Mr William Cox letting himself in at the office door, Mr Cole's carriage horses returning from exercise, or a stray letter-boy on an obstinate mule, were the liveliest objects she could presume to expect; and when her eyes fell only on the butcher with his tray, a tidy old woman travelling homewards from shop with her full baskets, two curs quarrelling over a dirty bone, and a string of children daudling round the baker's little bow-window eyeing the gingerbread, she knew she had no reason to complain, and was amused enough; quite enough still to stand at the door. A mind lively and at ease, can do with seeing nothing, and can see nothing that does not answer.[1]

'. . . her eyes fell *only*' on a whole miniature panorama and she is satisfied with seeing 'nothing'.

In *Persuasion*, the author gives a third-person summary of Captain Wentworth's first call at Uppercross Cottage.

> Mary, very much gratified by this attention, was delighted to receive him; while a thousand feelings rushed on Anne, of which this was the most consoling, that it would soon be over. And it was soon over. In two minutes after Charles's preparation, the others appeared; they were in the drawing-room. Her eye half met Captain Wentworth's; a bow, a curtsey passed; she heard his voice – he talked to Mary, said all that was right; said something to the Miss Musgroves, enough to mark an easy footing : the room seemed full – full of persons and voices – but a few minutes ended it.[2]

1. *Emma*, p. 233.

2. *Persuasion*, p. 59.

Ostensibly this is a description by a narrator, but it is told in such a way – with short sentences and clauses – that it suggests the breathlessness of Anne's own feelings as she sees her former fiancé for the first time in eight years. So Jane Austen not only enters directly into the mind of her heroine, but expresses herself much as Anne might, were she forced to describe the meeting herself.

In *Wuthering Heights* great complexity of point of view is achieved by reason of the fact that there are several layers of narration between the reader and the events: Mr Lockwood relates to the reader what he has heard from Nelly Dean and she in turn tells him of conversations she has had with Heathcliff, Cathy, and others. A similar situation exists in Conrad's novels. Distance is achieved, but it is of a different sort from that found in the drama; here, distortion is inevitable and deliberate; the action is refracted through several lenses, each of which is in some way limited as to its scope and power; the intermediary narrators thus act as unconscious commentators on the quality of the action described.

Robert Ferrars so describes his own feelings about the projected marriage between Lucy Steele and his brother, and relates something of the conversation with Mrs Ferrars on the subject.

'We may treat it as a joke,' said he at last, recovering from the affected laugh which had considerably lengthened out the genuine gaiety of the moment – 'but upon my soul it is a most serious business. Poor Edward! he is ruined for ever. I am extremely sorry for it – for I know him to be a very good-hearted creature; as well-meaning a fellow perhaps, as any in the world. You must not judge of him, Miss Dashwood, from *your* slight acquaintance. – Poor Edward! – His manners are certainly not the happiest in nature. – But we are not all born, you know, with the same powers – the same address.' [1]

The utter ridiculousness of Mrs Ferrars's (and Robert's) attitudes is underlined by the fact that he so fatuously reports the

1. *Sense and Sensibility*, p. 298.

incident – so extravagantly, and so foolishly. Yet there is another purpose to this conversation. Elinor feels that the marriage between Lucy and Edward will be a mistake, but the heroine's disapproval rests on quite different grounds from those of Mrs Ferrars and Robert: this conversation is an oblique comment in favour of Edward's faithfulness to his word, and as such must sharpen our respect for the young man.

It is equally true that other instances of such reportage show that the author has a definite purpose in mind in using this technique. Elinor Dashwood is apprised by Lucy herself of the latter's engagement to Edward Ferrars (*Sense and Sensibility*, I, xxii), and neither the heroine nor the reader is permitted to learn anything directly from Edward about the affair until very much later: the hero, as a man of honour, cannot disclose that his early attachment was made foolishly, while he is still engaged to the girl; Lucy Steele, on the other hand, reveals a great deal of herself by her manner in boasting of the engagement to Elinor; and the reader is left in suspense as to the true nature of the relationship until after Lucy has eloped with Robert Ferrars. Henry Tilney explains to Catherine Morland the reason for the General's turning her out (*Northanger Abbey*, II, xv): Jane Austen, as is well known, is unwilling to present a conversation between two men alone, unless there is a woman present; and the General must have explained to his son his disapprobation of a match to an unmoneyed girl, with an explicitness and directness impossible if the heroine were present. The early relationship between Fitzwilliam Darcy and George Wickham is never directly presented to the reader; the time scheme of the book forbids it: the action of *Pride and Prejudice* takes place long afterwards; but there are other important reasons: George Wickham gives the first version (I, xvi), which much maligns the squire of Pemberley – and so reinforces Elizabeth's prejudice; Darcy then, in the famous letter to Elizabeth (II, xii), gives the true version which discloses at once the measure of his honourable discretion, the softening of his pride, the unimpeachability of his behaviour to Wickham, and the strength of his affection for the girl.

In fact, letters provide a very effective method of indirect reportage. One remembers the complexity achieved towards the end of *Lord Jim*, when Marlow, back in London, learns of Jim's fate through the increasing faintness of several correspondents. So in Jane Austen, it is Miss Bennet who writes Elizabeth about Lydia and Wickham (*Pride and Prejudice*, III, iv). And in *Mansfield Park*, Fanny, at Portsmouth, gets the first hint of Henry Crawford's elopement with Maria, when she is importuned by Mary in a letter to ignore '"a most scandalous, ill-natured rumour"'.[1] Again, Robert Martin's proposal of marriage comes by letter – which, however, we never see; thus an additional level is interposed between the fact and the reader.

2. INDIRECT COMMENT

Jane Austen is, then, never more than ostensibly objective. When, however, she intrudes herself indirectly, she casts aside all pretence. While apparently proceeding along the lines laid out by the requirements of neutral narration, she often – by a word, a phrase, a personal note of qualification – discloses a view which cannot represent that of any of her characters, and which may not be her own.

When Sir John Middleton calls on the Dashwoods to invite them to meet Anne and Lucy Steele, the author cannot forbear to comment.

> Sir John wanted the whole family to walk to the Park directly and look at his guests. Benevolent, philanthropic man! It was painful to him even to keep a third cousin to himself.[2]

It is Jane Austen's voice which speaks, but are these her sentiments? The reader pauses over the descriptive exclamation, but then finds that it is intended ironically; for Sir John's

1. *Mansfield Park*, p. 437. 2. *Sense and Sensibility*, p. 119.

benevolence consists in giving cousins away. But is the statement meant simply to be reversed? If so, Sir John is a selfish man – and that cannot be, from what we know about him. No, his generosity is both large and undiscriminating; he thoroughly likes John Willoughby, simply because the latter is a good horseman and a tireless dancer. So Jane Austen indicates her qualified approval of the baronet, and the measure of her disapproval, by the oblique ironic description.

Mrs Allen, on arriving in Bath, is anxious to have a friend with whom she can talk, and soon she

> ... recognized the features of a former school-fellow and intimate, whom she had seen only once since their respective marriages, and that many years ago. Their joy on this meeting was very great, as well it might, since they had been contented to know nothing of each other for the last fifteen years.[1]

It is the author's voice which comments upon the encounter of Mrs Thorpe and Mrs Allen, but the very diction demands that the statement be read ironically. Jane Austen, we must suppose, will not deny the two ladies the pleasure of joy on this occasion; but she cannot forbear to suggest the superficiality of their friendship.

Catherine Morland is a long time outgrowing the Gothic illusions with which she has so assiduously equipped herself in her early youth; one of them is the sentimental confidante, who for her takes the shape of Isabella Thorpe. Catherine, whose basic good sense is indisputable, gradually has her eyes opened: when Isabella writes a hypocritical letter reasserting her attachment to James Morland – after a flirtation with Captain Tilney – the author comments: 'Such a strain of shallow artifice could not impose even upon Catherine.'[2] This is the remark of someone who was some distance from the immediate situation; as we have already seen, the peculiar *données* of *Northanger Abbey* require such detached observation.

In Derbyshire Elizabeth Bennet first awakens to the true

1. *Northanger Abbey*, pp. 31, 32. 2. ibid., p. 218.

nature of her sentiment for Darcy – but she is called away suddenly on account of the elopement of Lydia and Wickham. She hates to go, and she 'sighed at the perverseness of those feelings which would now have promoted its continuance [their acquaintance] and would formerly have rejoiced in its termination'. Then the author steps in:

> If gratitude and esteem are good foundations of affection, Elizabeth's change of sentiment will be neither improbable nor faulty. But if otherwise, if the regard springing from such sources is unreasonable or unnatural, in comparison of what is so often described as arising on a first interview with its object, and even before two words have been exchanged, nothing can be said in her defence, except that she had given somewhat of a trial to the latter method, in her partiality for Wickham, and that its ill-success might perhaps authorise her to seek the other less interesting mode of attachment. Be that as it may, she saw him go with regret....[1]

This passage is sometimes cited to indicate Jane Austen's alleged want of passion; but it can be misleading only if the reader forgets the rest of the novel, during which there is a great deal of time for Elizabeth's incipient affection to turn to ardent love. Deep within Jane Austen, as the delineation of Wickham shows, is a distrust of appearance; and Elizabeth has learned from her experience with the Meryton lieutenant to look beyond surface to essence, so it is natural that she should not fling herself immediately at Darcy; it is inevitable, in the terms of the story itself, that 'gratitude and esteem' should be now more highly valued by her: but they do not preclude love.

The strict (and rather narrow) moralizing tone of *Mansfield Park* stems in part from the frequent indirect comment by the author. After Mrs Norris had confirmed the Miss Bertrams' impression that Fanny is stupid because she does not know or '"want to learn either music or drawing"', the author introduces a sharp comment:

> Such were the counsels by which Mrs Norris assisted to form her nieces' minds; and it is not very wonderful that with all their

1. *Pride and Prejudice*, p. 279.

promising talents and early information, they should be entirely deficient in the less common acquirements of self-knowledge, generosity, and humility. In every thing but disposition, they were admirably taught.[1]

Sir Thomas Bertram, after returning from Antigua, finds that he disapproves of James Rushworth, the fiancé of his elder daughter, and so he offers to break off the engagement for her, for he believes – correctly – that she does not love the young man. She refuses, however, and the author interprets the refusal.

Had Sir Thomas applied to his daughter within the first three or four days after Henry Crawford's leaving Mansfield, before her feelings were at all tranquillized, before she had given up every hope of him, or absolutely resolved on enduring his rival, her answer might have been different; but after another three or four days, when there was no return, no letter, no message – no symptom of a softened heart – no hope of advantage from separation – her mind became cool enough to seek all the comfort that pride and self-revenge could give.[2]

This is a paragraph of severe moral censure, of elucidation which could not be made by any person in the story itself; it has no flavour of the gaiety which informs the comment of her first three novels; in the last two, her indirect comment is to be no less serious – but not quite so solemn.

Emma Woodhouse's faults are described with a sly understatement which does not detract from the general radiance of tone of the novel, but which nevertheless is meant to announce the problem of the story: '... *rather* too much her own way', a '*little* too well of herself', 'so unperceived', and 'rank as misfortunes': this is the diction of irony, forcing by its understatement a close examination of what Emma thinks and does in the book, to show evidence of the truth of this criticism.

Again, Jane Austen tells us about Mrs Goddard:

Mrs Goddard was the mistress of a School – not of a seminary, or an establishment, or any thing which professed, in long sentences

1. *Mansfield Park*, p. 19. 2. ibid., pp. 201, 202.

of refined nonsense, to combine liberal requirements with elegant morality upon new principles and new systems – and where young ladies for enormous pay might be screwed out of health and into vanity – but a real, honest, old-fashioned Boarding-school, where a reasonable quantity of accomplishments were sold at a reasonable price, and where girls might be sent to be out of the way and scramble themselves into a little education, without any danger of coming back prodigies.[1]

If the reader is not sufficiently acquainted with Jane Austen to know of her complete distrust of elegant diction – or rather, the humbug that lies behind it – this passage will be a sufficient introduction to the fact. The contrast drawn between the two kinds of school is heightened by the author's use of simple – even vulgar – words to describe the common-sense 'establishment' over which Mrs Goddard presides.

At Box Hill Emma behaves very badly – unconscionably, censurably, in her flirtation with Frank Churchill:

> Not that Emma was gay and thoughtless from any real felicity; it was rather because she felt less happy than she had expected. She laughed because she was disappointed; and though she liked him for his attentions, and thought them all, whether in friendship, admiration, or playfulness, extremely judicious, they were not winning back her heart. She still intended him for her friend.[2]

Much is told here from the viewpoint of the heroine – but a moment's reflection will disclose that there is a subtle piece of analysis in this passage of which Emma herself is not yet capable: Jane Austen wishes to inform us, by an indirect intrusion, of the exact reason for Emma's behaviour on this occasion, and this is one of her author's nicest pieces of psychological insight.

When at last Emma realizes that she has been unconsciously in love with Mr Knightley all along, she reflects at length on the matter, especially after his proposal of marriage. The author interrupts very briefly to say:

1. *Emma*, pp. 21, 22. 2. ibid., p. 368.

> It is remarkable, that Emma, in the many, very many, points of view in which she was now beginning to consider Donwell Abbey, was never struck with any sense of injury to her nephew Henry, whose rights as heir expectant had formerly been so tenaciously regarded. Think she must of the possible difference to the poor little boy; and yet she only gave herself a saucy conscious smile about it, and found amusement in detecting the real cause of that violent dislike of Mr Knightley's marrying Jane Fairfax, or any body else, which at the time she had wholly imputed to the amiable solicitude of the sister and the aunt.[1]

Little Henry is throughout much of the novel a symbol of Emma's self-delusion; when the author calls it 'remarkable' that her heroine 'was never struck with any sense of injury to him', she is speaking with an irony which must help to measure the distance Emma has gone since the beginning of the story.

After a narration of the facts of the early love between Anne Elliot and Captain Wentworth, their author makes a rather subtle point:

> How eloquent could Anne Elliot have been, – how eloquent, at least, were her wishes on the side of early warm attachment, and a cheerful confidence in futurity, against that over-anxious caution which seems to insult exertion and distrust Providence! – She had been forced into prudence in her youth, she learned romance as she grew older – the natural sequel of an unnatural beginning.[2]

The last sentence in this paragraph has a detached and summary quality; it is obviously the remark of some one other than the heroine. It is in fact Jane Austen speaking, and with a high seriousness which cannot be doubted if the context is taken into account; the statement tells by implication of the increasing weight which the author is putting upon the value of love: for we must infer that if one commits oneself 'on the side of early warm attachment', the *natural* sequel will be prudential.

1. ibid., pp. 449, 450. 2. *Persuasion*, p. 30.

3. DIRECT COMMENT

Sometimes (though quite infrequently) Jane Austen insinuates herself into the narrative *in propria persona*, yet even when she uses the first personal pronoun the reader must beware lest he be led, by this close intimacy, into thinking that what is being said represents the view of the author. The 'I' is occasionally Jane Austen herself, but not by any means always.

In the second volume of *Sense and Sensibility*, the author begins a paragraph in this manner: 'I come now to the relation of a misfortune, which about this time befell Mrs John Dashwood.' [1] The 'I' is not Jane Austen: for the 'misfortune' is that Fanny Dashwood has invited Elinor and Marianne to a musical party because she wants to invite Lady Middleton, and is under the mistaken impression that the two sisters are the latter's house-guests. The author cannot think it unfortunate that Mrs John Dashwood should show some attention to her sisters-in-law, but she identifies herself with that selfish woman in order to strengthen the case against her. By itself, this example is not deeply significant: the context of the paragraph makes perfectly clear the fact that a simple ironic reversal is all that is called for; the reader needs only reflect briefly on the train of causation to know that moral censure of Fanny Dashwood is being implied. But because it is apparent that the 'I' is not Jane Austen, the reader can therefore look more critically at other passages wherein he might simply assume that the use of the first personal pronoun automatically indicates the viewpoint of the author.

How, for instance, shall we interpret the long passage in defence of the novel, in *Northanger Abbey*? Jane Austen tells us that Isabella Thorpe and Catherine often 'read novels together'.

> Yes, novels; for I will not adopt that ungenerous and impolitic custom so common with novel writers, of degrading by their con-

1. *Sense and Sensibility*, p. 248. See also pp. 368, 376, 378.

temptuous censure the very performances, to the number of which they are themselves adding – joining with their greatest enemies in bestowing the harshest epithets on such works, and scarcely ever permitting them to be read by their own heroine, who, if she accidentally take up a novel, is sure to turn over its insipid pages with disgust. Alas! if the heroine of one novel be not patronized by the heroine of another, from whom can she expect protection and regard? I cannot approve of it. Let us leave it to the Reviewers to abuse such effusions of fancy at their leisure, and over every new novel to talk in threadbare strains of the trash with which the press now groans. Let us not desert one another; we are an injured body. Although our productions have afforded more extensive and unaffected pleasure than those of any other literary corporation in the world, no species of composition has been so much decried. From pride, ignorance, or fashion, our foes are almost as many as our readers. And while the abilities of the nine-hundredth abridger of the History of England, or of the man who collects and publishes in a volume some dozen lines of Milton, Pope, and Prior, with a paper from the Spectator, and a chapter from Sterne, are eulogized by a thousand pens, – there seems almost a general wish of decrying the capacity and undervaluing the labour of the novelist, and of slighting the performances which have only genius, wit, and taste to recommend them. 'I am no novel reader – I seldom look into novels – Do not imagine that *I* often read novels – It is really very well for a novel.' – Such is the common cant. – 'And what are you reading, Miss —?' 'Oh! it is only a novel!' replies the young lady; while she lays down her book with affected indifference, or momentary shame. – 'It is only Cecilia, or Camilla, or Belinda'; or, in short, only some work in which the greatest powers of the mind are displayed, in which the most thorough knowledge of human nature, the happiest delineation of its varieties, the liveliest effusions of wit and humour are conveyed to the world in the best chosen language. Now, had the same young lady been engaged with a volume of the Spectator, instead of such a work, how proudly would she have produced the book, and told its name; though the chances must be against her being occupied by any part of that voluminous publication, of which either the matter or manner would not disgust a young person of taste. . . .[1]

1. *Northanger Abbey*, pp. 37, 38.

In interpreting this passage the reader must keep in mind the fact that *Northanger Abbey* is a burlesque and that in this particular chapter Jane Austen has been making a good deal of fun of both her heroine and Isabella Thorpe. For, although it is clear that Jane Austen is attacking reviewers, there is, as Miss Lascelles suggests (she does not develop the point), 'some suspicion of overstatement, pendant to the demure understatement in Catherine's eventual criticism of Mrs Radcliffe'.[1] We know that Jane Austen likes the author of *Belinda*, for she tells her niece, 'I have made up my mind to like no Novels really, but Miss Edgeworth's Yours & my own.' And her admiration for Madame d'Arblay is also well known. She does not mention Mrs Radcliffe here, and *The Mysteries of Udolpho* is what she is principally satirizing in *Northanger Abbey*. Furthermore, Jane Austen is a delightedly satiric 'abridger' of Goldsmith's *History of England*. On the other hand there is the suspicious orotundity of diction and of sentiment in the extravagant praise which she gives to novels and novelists: 'genius, wit, and taste', Jane Austen's own reading and writing show, are (in her opinion) not nearly always present in the novel. There is the doubtless more palpable fact that our author was an enthusiastic reader of the eighteenth-century essayists, of whom she here speaks so slightingly – though she parodies Dr Johnson at times, she thinks him 'dear', and, according to her brother, Johnson was her favourite moral writer in prose.[2] It may thus be that the entire passage is ironic, in that it displays an ambivalent attitude toward her subject matter.

Tongue in cheek, she draws the moral of *Northanger Abbey*:

1. Mary Lascelles, *Jane Austen and Her Art*, p. 49.

2. *Letters*, II, 405 (28 September 1814); for her references to Fanny Burney see the 'Index to Literary Allusions', *Northanger Abbey*, p. 297, *s.v.* 'Burney'; for Jane Austen as essay-reader see Miss Lascelles, op. cit., Chap. II, *passim*; see Henry Austen's 'Biographical Notice of the Author', reprinted in the Chapman edition of *Northanger Abbey*, p. 7; see also Dr Chapman's remarks in the 'Index of Literary Allusions', ibid., pp. 299, 300, *s.v.* 'Johnson'.

> To begin perfect happiness at the respective ages of twenty-six and eighteen, is to do pretty well; and professing myself moreover convinced, that the General's unjust interference, so far from being really injurious to their felicity, was perhaps rather conducive to it, by improving their knowledge of each other, and adding strength to their attachment, I leave it to be settled by whomsoever it may concern, whether the tendency of this work be altogether to recommend parental tyranny, or reward filial disobedience.[1]

The two alternatives proffered actually have nothing to do with the 'tendency' of *Northanger Abbey*, which is partly to expose through burlesque the Gothic delusions, and partly to display with irony the human condition of *naïveté*: the General and his disapprobation are really a most exterior aspect of the plot; the reader realizes this and is led by the author's spurious moralizing to reflect on the true significance of the book.

Many people have overlooked the significance of the following sentences from *Mansfield Park*; they occur at the beginning of the final chapter. Maria Bertram has run away with Henry Crawford, Tom Bertram is ill, Julia has eloped to Scotland with Yates – and everyone else (except Mary Crawford) is angry or disappointed or both.

> Let other pens dwell on guilt and misery. I quit such odious subjects as soon as I can, impatient to restore every body, not greatly in fault themselves, to tolerable comfort, and to have done with all the rest.[2]

Most critics have accepted this statement at its face value and adduced it in favour of a theory that Jane Austen is not interested in or concerned with this side of life. But we have learned to distrust statements which Jane Austen makes, even in her own person. Besides, as Dr Chapman points out with reference to 'guilt and misery', 'She in fact dwells on them

1. *Northanger Abbey*, p. 252. 2. *Mansfield Park*, p. 461.

herself, briefly but adequately.')[1] And, as he does not point out, Jane Austen in this very chapter more nearly approaches the boundaries of tragedy than in any other part of her work: it is Sir Thomas Bertram's self-castigating moment of awareness when he reflects on his duties as a parent.

> He feared that principle, active principle, had been wanting, that they had never been properly taught to govern their inclinations and tempers, by that sense of duty which can alone suffice. They had been instructed theoretically in their religion, but never required to bring it into daily practice. To be distinguished for elegance and accomplishments – the authorized object of their youth – could have had no useful influence that way, no moral effect on the mind. He had meant them to be good, but his cares had been directed to the understanding and manners, not the disposition; and of the necessity of self-denial and humility, he feared they had never heard from any lips that could profit them.
>
> Bitterly did he deplore a deficiency which now he could scarcely comprehend to have been possible. Wretchedly did he feel, that with all the cost and care of an anxious and expensive education, he had brought up his daughters without their understanding their first duties, or his being acquainted with their character and temper.[2]

We must, then, I think read the 'guilt and misery' sentences ironically – as the expression of a wish which cannot be fulfilled, rather than as a statement of fact.

1. R. W. Chapman, *Jane Austen Facts and Problems*, p. 195. Miss Husbands has suggested to me that Dr Chapman is no doubt using 'dwells' in a different sense from Jane Austen. For she *deals with* 'guilt and misery', 'briefly but adequately'; what Jane Austen says is that she does not linger over them longer than necessary. This seems to me a more accurate comment than Dr Chapman's; but it hardly lessens the force of contrast in what follows on Jane Austen's disclaimer.

2. *Mansfield Park*, pp. 463, 464.

4. THE 'UNIVERSALLY ACKNOWLEDGED TRUTH'

Related to the personal and impersonal intrusion by the author is her penchant for sprinkling maxims in her works – or rather sayings that seem to have the authority of maxims but which may have little weight so far as Jane Austen's own thinking is concerned. Actually, maxims usually express the common-sense point of view; and Jane Austen is full of that kind of sense – but she goes far beyond it; and hovering about every single piece of homely wisdom is the ironic qualification.

The Miss Steeles win their way to Lady Middleton's approbation through the ancient device of paying attention to her children.

> Fortunately for those who pay their court through such foibles, a fond mother, though, in pursuit of praise for her children, the most rapacious of human beings, is likewise the most credulous; her demands are exorbitant; but she will swallow any thing; and the excessive affection and endurance of the Miss Steeles towards her offspring, were viewed therefore by Lady Middleton without the smallest surprise or distrust.[1]

The tone here indicates a generalization based upon much experience, the fruit of much observation of mothers and their children; yet the extravagance of 'rapacious' and 'she will swallow any thing' suggests that this statement is both true and not true, that it may be an oblique comment on the fatuousness of Lady Middleton and the hypocrisy of the Miss Steeles.

Lucy Steele, having eloped with Robert Ferrars, is at last restored to the good graces of Mrs Ferrars.

> The whole of Lucy's behaviour in the affair, and the prosperity which crowned it, therefore, may be held forth as a most encouraging instance of what an earnest, an unceasing attention to self-interest, however its progress may be apparently obstructed, will do in securing every advantage of fortune, with no other sacrifice than that of time and conscience.[2]

1. *Sense and Sensibility*, p. 120. 2. ibid., p. 376.

Does Jane Austen here mean to 'encourage' the reader? Obviously not, for while she candidly admits the truth that sometimes 'an unceasing attention to self-interest' will bring material rewards, her very overstatement makes the reader stop and ponder – and the entire intention is given away by the fact that conscience must be sacrificed.

Speaking of Catherine and Henry Tilney, Jane Austen writes:

> Catherine ... did not know that a good-looking girl, with an affectionate heart and a very ignorant mind, cannot fail of attracting a clever young man, unless circumstances are particularly untoward.[1]

Catherine is indeed good-looking, affectionate, and ignorant – but she is more besides: she is intelligent, sweet-tempered, and honest; and it is to the whole of her personality and attributes that Henry Tilney responds; so that this 'maxim' in its context and by the unqualifiedness of its 'cannot fail' shows the very limitations of the common sense which it pretends to exhibit.

In fact, about common sense itself Jane Austen constructs a generalization which by the simplicity of its diction and the power of its context demands acceptance. Catherine Morland, having been evicted without stated cause from Northanger Abbey, returns home, where she finds sympathy but not much understanding of her painful situation. Mrs Morland talks sensibly to her daughter, and

> There was a great deal of good sense in all this; but there are some situations of the human mind in which good sense has very little power; and Catherine's feelings contradicted almost every position her mother advanced.[2]

Mrs Morland has, of course, hardly understood her daughter's position: she speaks sensibly of the facts which she does understand. But Catherine, wounded not only by her dismissal but by a more thorough and more anguishing knowledge of the facts of the case, is in no mood to react sensibly. The facts are not reasonable. Not that Jane Austen's cautious and quali-

1. *Northanger Abbey*, p. 111.   2. ibid., p. 239.

fied maxim is meant to deny the values of good sense, only to indicate that it has limits.

There is also, of course, the famous first sentence of *Pride and Prejudice*, from which this section has received its name: 'It is a truth universally acknowledged, that a single man in possession of a good fortune, must be in want of a wife.' That this statement is meant to have ironic qualification is shown both in the orotundity of the diction, and by contrast with what is said in the following sentence – that the concern is to be not with the universe but with a 'neighbourhood', not with the totality of mankind, but with 'the surrounding families'.

After Mr Knightley has proposed to Emma and been accepted, he relates something to his new fiancée about the nature and history of his feelings for her. Jane Austen interposes:

> Seldom, very seldom, does complete truth belong to any human disclosure; seldom can it happen that something is not a little disguised, or a little mistaken. . . .[1]

There is a wryness in the generalization, achieved no doubt through the use of the word 'little' twice: for the book has been about the grand disguises and the enormous mistakes in interpretation which have, by their eventual disclosure, educated Emma.

'Seldom ... does complete truth belong to any human disclosure –' even to Jane Austen's, and especially when she adopts the role of a phrase-maker whose aphorisms seem to sum up experience. For she knows that life is more complex than any adage will allow, that any simple 'truth' is two-edged, that black can as often be proved white as black.

5. THE DRAMATIC MODE

Very much of Jane Austen's work is in dialogue form; she is a master-dramatist – with a perfect ear, a perfect sense of

1. *Emma*, p. 431.

timing, a shrewd instinct for climax and anti-climax. And when one thinks of Jane Austen's novels one is apt to remember most clearly such conversations as that between Mr and Mrs Bennet on the subject of the new tenant at Netherfield Park (*Pride and Prejudice*, I, i), or the dialogue in which Mrs John Dashwood dissuades her husband from doing anything beyond giving nominal offers of assistance to his stepmother and half-sisters (*Sense and Sensibility*, I, ii), or Sir Walter Elliot's animadversions on the Navy as a career (*Persuasion*, I, iii).

In the drama, irony proceeds as Sedgewick points out, from 'the sense of contradiction felt by spectators of a drama who see a character acting in ignorance of his condition'.[1] Thus in the dialogues of Jane Austen just mentioned, Mrs Bennet is ignorant (as always) that her husband is making not very subtle fun of her; John Dashwood is quite unaware that his first instinct of generosity is being whittled down bit by bit, until virtually nothing is left; and Sir Walter's objections to the Navy are seen (though not by him) to be compounded partly of enormous snobbery and partly of a vanity of appearance which would make him unwilling to expose his face to the salty breezes of the sea. But let us look with close attention at one particularly ironic dialogue, that between Lady Catherine de Bourgh and Elizabeth Bennet, on the subject of Mr Darcy.

'You can be at no loss, Miss Bennet, to understand the reason of my journey hither. Your own heart, your own conscience, must tell you why I come.'

Elizabeth looked with unaffected astonishment.

'Indeed, you are mistaken, Madam. I have not been at all able to account for the honour of seeing you here.'

'Miss Bennet,' replied her ladyship, in an angry tone, 'you ought to know, that I am not to be trifled with. But however insincere *you* may choose to be, you shall not find *me* so. My character has ever been celebrated for its sincerity and frankness, and in a cause of such moment as this, I shall certainly not depart from it. A

1. G. G. Sedgewick, *Of Irony* . . . , p. 43.

report of a most alarming nature, reached me two days ago. I was told, that not only your sister was on the point of being most advantageously married, but that *you*, that Miss Elizabeth Bennet, would, in all likelihood, be soon afterwards united to my nephew, my own nephew, Mr Darcy. Though I *know* it must be a scandalous falsehood; though I would not injure him so much as to suppose the truth of it possible, I instantly resolved on setting off for this place, that I might make my sentiments known to you.' [1]

Lady Catherine's self-ignorance is colossal: she *is* to be trifled with, her 'sincerity and frankness' are immediately impugned, when Elizabeth retorts,

'If you believed it impossible to be true ... I wonder you took the trouble of coming so far. What could your ladyship propose by it?' [2]

The conversation results in a complete rout for Lady Catherine – she goes away '"most seriously displeased"', having failed to exact any promise from Elizabeth not to marry Darcy. Retrospectively, this interchange gains in irony, for we learn in the concluding pages that the heroine's refusal to make such a promise to Lady Catherine is reported by Her Ladyship to Darcy himself – and this gives strength to his hope that he might be accepted.

We cannot leave off consideration of Jane Austen's dramatic instinct without giving attention to her technique of abbreviating long conversations which by their compression make for a greater ironic impact than would otherwise be possible. Much of what Miss Bates says is so condensed, but perhaps the most delightful example is that of Mrs Elton at Donwell Abbey:

The whole party were assembled, excepting Frank Churchill, who was expected every moment from Richmond; and Mrs Elton, in all her apparatus of happiness, her large bonnet and her basket, was very ready to lead the way in gathering, accepting, or talking – strawberries, and only strawberries, could now be thought or

1. *Pride and Prejudice*, p. 353. This conversation continues through p. 358.

2. ibid., p. 353.

spoken of. – 'The best fruit in England – every body's favourite – always wholesome. – These the finest beds and finest sorts. – Delightful to gather for one's self – the only way of really enjoying them. – Morning decidedly the best time – never tired – every sort good – hautboy infinitely superior – no comparison – the others hardly eatable – hautboys very scarce – Chili preferred – white wood finest flavour of all – price of strawberries in London – abundance about Bristol – Maple Grove – cultivation – beds when to be renewed – gardeners thinking exactly different – no general rule – gardeners never to be put out of their way – delicious fruit – only too rich to be eaten much of – inferior to cherries – currants more refreshing – only objection to gathering strawberries the stooping – glaring sun – tired to death – could bear it no longer – must go and sit in the shade.' [1]

We can almost see Mrs Elton, back and logic bending, bending, bending. But the whole vivid scene is presented to us (in the manner Boswell sometimes uses) dramatically, in an abbreviated monologue.

Closely related to the dramatic mode of presentation is indirect discourse – the more or less verbatim report, in the third person, of a conversation. I suspect that Jane Austen used this technique for two purposes: first, to abbreviate what would otherwise be rather tediously conventional dialogues; second, to present verbal interchanges which she cannot quite trust her ear to reproduce exactly.[2]

Of the first type is the conversation of Mrs Palmer on arriving at Berkeley Street to call on Mrs Jennings and the Miss Dashwoods.

They had not long finished their breakfast before Mrs Palmer's barouche stopt at the door, and in a few minutes she came laughing into the room; so delighted to see them all, that it was hard

1. *Emma*, pp. 358, 359.

2. The reader will at once be struck with the similarity of this technique to that of the 'Objective' Account. But there is the important difference that in indirect discourse some real effort is made to echo the diction and syntax of the persons involved. In the 'Objective' Account the prose style is, as it were, 'neutral'.

to say whether she received most pleasure from meeting her mother or the Miss Dashwoods again. So surprised at their coming to town, though it was what she had rather expected all along; so angry at their accepting her mother's invitation after having declined her own, though at the same time she would never have forgiven them if they had not come![1]

For a similar reason Jane Austen so reports William Collins's conversation with Mrs Bennet, on his first visit to Longbourn:

He had not been long seated before he complimented Mrs Bennett on having so fine a family of daughters, said he had heard much of their beauty, but that, in this instance, fame had fallen short of the truth; and added, that he did not doubt her seeing them all in due time well disposed of in marriage.[2]

The subject of marriage proposals in Jane Austen's novels is an interesting one: never does she present dramatically the conversation in which the betrothal is made. In *Sense and Sensibility* both proposals of marriage are related quasi-objectively by the author, as is Henry's proposal to Catherine in *Northanger Abbey*. In *Pride and Prejudice*, most of Mr Darcy's first proposal is presented by means of indirect discourse; the second is preceded by directly reported conversation, but the mutual declarations themselves are simply narrated. Emma Woodhouse's two offers of marriage follow exactly the same pattern as that set by *Pride and Prejudice*, while in *Mansfield Park* both proposals occur very much off-stage; and in *Persuasion* Captain Wentworth declares himself in a letter. The technique of indirect discourse does not serve any ironic function, except in so far as the compression involved makes it similar to the abbreviated direct conversation discussed above: this method saves Jane Austen the inaccuracy of reporting directly what she cannot hear clearly.

1. *Sense and Sensibility*, p. 164. 2. *Pride and Prejudice*, pp. 64. 65.

6. INTERIOR DISCLOSURES

Fiction has an advantage over life in being more completely revealing: truer, as poetry is truer than history. In the novel we see people's thoughts and imaginings without the colorations of fear, reserve, and diffidence, which in life constitute effective barriers against the disclosure of personality. In life we can hardly know ourselves, let alone anyone else; in fiction we can understand people as in no other medium – not even the drama, which has to depend more on action than does the novel. It may be that one reason why Jane Austen abandoned the epistolary form, which she used in *Love and Freindship* and *Elinor and Marianne* (not to mention *Volume the First*), is that it enjoins the author to so exterior a presentation by limiting the letter-writer to a few correspondents, all of them inhibited by the restraints laid upon that aspect of human intercourse: even *Werther*, with all its effusions, suffers thus from being written in letter form. In any event – and with an omniscience which now seems old-fashioned to the followers of Henry James – Jane Austen allows us to see within the minds not only of her heroines but of many other characters as well.

Newton Arvin has remarked that the Henry Adams of the *Education* is very different from the man of the *Letters*; the autobiography is, whether consciously or unconsciously (it does not matter), a dramatic re-formation of the events of his life: in the *Education*, Adams 'simplified, distorted, and misrepresented his own intellectual and emotional past'.[1] And anyone perusing Boswell's *London Journal* will observe the difference between the young man's description of his first meeting with Johnson and the account which appears in the *Life*. This is to say – and it has been said before – that even biography, however honest it attempts to be, does not with complete accuracy describe its subject – it is a work of art, and no human being is a work of art. It should follow, then,

1. Newton Arvin, Introduction to *Selected Letters of Henry Adams*, New York, 1951, p. 21.

that fiction is probably a less accurate portrait of the artist. Yet attempts are frequently made to identify Jane Austen with her fictional people – to impute to their author the characteristics of her heroines.[1] But Elinor and Marianne Dashwood, Catherine Morland, Elizabeth Bennet, Fanny Price, Emma Woodhouse, and Anne Elliot are such different people that it is hard to imagine them yoked together in one personality, however many facets that personality may have. Besides, no one would suppose that the following reflections represent the thinking of Jane Austen:

The Tilneys, they, by whom above all, she desired to be favourably thought of, outstripped even her wishes in the flattering measures by which their intimacy was to be continued. She was to be their chosen visitor, she was to be for weeks under the same roof with the person whose society she mostly prized – and, in addition to all the rest, this roof was to be the roof of an abbey! – Her passion for ancient edifices was next in degree to her passion for Henry Tilney – and castles and abbies made usually the charm of those reveries which his image did not fill. To see and explore either the ramparts and keep of the one, or the cloisters of the other, had been for many weeks a darling wish, though to be more than the visitor of an hour, had seemed too nearly impossible for desire. And yet, this was to happen. With all the chances against her of house, hall, place, park, court, and cottage, Northanger turned up an abbey, and she was to be its inhabitant. Its long, damp passages, its narrow cells and ruined chapel, were to be within her daily reach, and she could not entirely subdue the hope of some traditional legends, some awful memorials of an injured and ill-fated nun.[2]

Nor could any reader for a moment be deluded, as Emma is in her thoughts on Mrs Weston's remarks about Mr Knightley and Jane Fairfax:

[Emma's] objections to Mr Knightley's marrying did not in the least subside. She could see nothing but evil in it. It would be a

1. Even Virginia Woolf does this, in an otherwise perceptive and sensitive essay, 'Jane Austen at Sixty', *New Republic*, XXXVII (1924), p. 261.

2. *Northanger Abbey*, p. 141.

great disappointment to Mr John Knightley; consequently to Isabella. A real injury to the children – a most mortifying change, and material loss to them all; – a very great deduction from her father's daily comfort – and, as to herself, she could not at all endure the idea of Jane Fairfax at Donwell Abbey. A Mrs Knightley for them all to give way to! – No – Mr Knightley must never marry. Little Henry must remain the heir of Donwell.[1]

But such obvious, and by no means infrequent, instances of separation between author and heroine are ignored – or passed over – by critics who would commit the autobiographical fallacy. They concentrate upon Elinor Dashwood, Elizabeth Bennet, and Anne Elliot – and sometimes poor little Fanny Price. Actually, however, Jane Austen dissociates herself even from these heroines, although she is at the same time intensely sympathetic with the 'goosish' Catherine Morland and the spoilt Emma Woodhouse. Altogether, Jane Austen maintains some distance without which irony would be impossible.

To take a rather difficult example, there is Elinor's reaction to the letter which Willoughby has written to Marianne:

With what indignation such a letter as this must be read by Miss Dashwood, may be imagined. Though aware, before she began it, that it must bring a confession of his inconstancy, and confirm their separation for ever, she was not aware that such language could be suffered to announce it; nor could she have supposed Willoughby capable of departing so far from the appearance of every honourable and delicate feeling – so far from the common decorum of a gentleman, as to send a letter so impudently cruel: a letter which, instead of bringing with his desire of a release any professions of regret, acknowledged no breach of faith, denied all peculiar affection whatever – a letter of which every line was an insult, and which proclaimed its writer to be deep in hardened villainy.[2]

This is a natural reaction, perhaps an inevitable one, but it is not Jane Austen's final word on Willoughby, whose penitent confession later moves even the presently infuriated Elinor

1. *Emma*, pp. 227, 228. 2. *Sense and Sensibility*, pp. 183, 184.

to compassion and forgiveness (*Sense and Sensibility*, III, viii).

One sign of a distance between Jane Austen and her heroines is found in the arrangement of their thought patterns – a slight abridgement takes place, perhaps some clarification as well, so that the reader can grasp what the heroine does not. There are, for example, Elizabeth Bennet's slowly self-modified impressions of Darcy's letter:

> Her feelings as she read were scarcely to be defined. With amazement did she first understand that he believed any apology to be in his power; and stedfastly was she persuaded that he could have no explanation to give, which a just sense of shame would not conceal. With a strong prejudice against everything he might say, she began his account of what had happened at Netherfield. She read, with an eagerness which hardly left her power of comprehension, and from impatience of knowing what the next sentence might bring was incapable of attending to the sense of the one before her eyes. His belief of her sister's insensibility, she instantly resolved to be false, and his account of the real, the worst objections to the match, made her too angry to have any wish of doing him justice. He expressed no regret for what he had done which satisfied her; his style was not penitent, but haughty. It was all pride and insolence.
>
> But when this subject was succeeded by his account of Mr Wickham, when she read with somewhat clearer attention a relation of events, which, if true, must overthrow every cherished opinion of his worth, and which bore so alarming an affinity to his own history of himself, her feelings were yet more acutely painful and more difficult of definition. Astonishment, apprehension, and even horror, oppressed her. She wished to discredit it entirely, repeatedly exclaiming, 'this must be false! This cannot be! This must be the grossest falsehood!' – and when she had gone through the whole letter, though scarcely knowing anything of the last page or two, put it hastily away, protesting that she would not regard it, that she would never look in it again.
>
> In this perturbed state of mind, with thoughts that could rest on nothing, she walked on; but it would not do; in half a minute the letter was unfolded again, and collecting herself as well as she could, she again began the mortifying perusal of all that related

to Wickham, and commanded herself so far as to examine the meaning of every sentence. . . . She put down the letter, weighed every circumstance with what she meant to be impartiality – deliberated on the probability of each statement – but with little success. On both sides it was only assertion. Again she read on. But every line proved more clearly that the affair, which she had believed it impossible that any contrivance could so represent, as to render Mr Darcy's conduct in it less than infamous, was capable of a turn which must make him entirely blameless throughout the whole.[1]

The sequence of thought here is evidently more obvious to the reader than to Elizabeth herself – from disdainful disbelief to somewhat reluctant acceptance. This is artistic objectivity. Such a sequence is more obviously adopted in Mr Knightley's quick changes of opinion about Frank Churchill as the squire proposes to, and is accepted by, Emma:

He had found her agitated and low. – Frank Churchill was a villain. – He heard her declare that she had never loved him. Frank Churchill's character was not desperate. – She was his own Emma, by hand and word, when they returned to the house; and if he could have thought of Frank Churchill then, he might have deemed him a very good sort of fellow.[2]

But Jane Austen is quite willing to take us into the minds of characters whom she cannot possibly resemble, and to whom she is unsympathetic. Any novelist worth his salt is bound to do so: and this fact in itself, which is obvious to any reader of fiction, simply supports the argument that the writer and his creations cannot be closely identified. For instance, Mary Crawford, on finding Tom Bertram indifferent to her after his return to Mansfield following a brief absence, finds 'his indifference . . . so much more than equalled by her own, that were he now to step forth the owner of Mansfield Park, the Sir Thomas complete, which he was to be in time, she did not believe she could accept him'.[3] And then there are Maria and Julia Bertram, of whose vacuous minds we get a glimpse:

1. *Pride and Prejudice*, pp. 204, 205. 2. *Emma*, p. 433.
3. *Mansfield Park*, p. 114.

Maria, with only Mr Rushworth to attend her, and doomed to the repeated details of his day's sport, good or bad, his boast of his dogs, his jealousy of his neighbours, his doubts of their qualification, and his zeal after poachers – subjects which will not find their way to female feelings without some talent on one side, or some attachment on the other, had missed Mr Crawford grievously; and Julia, unengaged and unemployed, felt all the right of missing him much more. Each sister believed herself the favourite.[1]

There are a dozen and one other examples: Sir Thomas Bertram, Charlotte Lucas, and Sir Walter Elliot, for instance.

Besides, Jane Austen's very omniscience argues that a single point of view could not comprehend the intent of the novels fully: the many shifts in viewpoint indicate a completeness and a detachment which none of the characters can possibly share. For instance, Elizabeth Bennet is unable to apprehend the true nature of Darcy's feelings for her until some time *after* his open declaration of love; the declaration itself is a stunning surprise – but not to the reader, who has already glimpsed the progress of the hero's feelings. Thus, very early in the story, while Jane Bennet languishes ill at Netherfield Park, Darcy reacts as follows to Elizabeth:

Though he had detected with a critical eye more than one failure of perfect symmetry in her form, he was forced to acknowledge her figure to be light and pleasing; and in spite of his asserting that her manners were not those of the fashionable world, he was caught by their easy playfulness. Of this she was perfectly unaware. . . .[2]

Again, after a verbal interchange, Darcy 'began to feel the danger of paying Elizabeth too much attention'.[3] But this is the technique of dramatic irony, which can more conveniently be dealt with in another chapter.

1. ibid., p. 115. 2. *Pride and Prejudice*, p. 23. 3. ibid., p. 58.

CHAPTER III

Heroines, Heroes, and Villains

JUST as Jane Austen depends on more than a single viewpoint for the exposition of her themes, so does her 'commanding centre' focus upon interrelationships between characters rather than upon a single individual. Every person has a function, yet everyone comes alive; even Lady Bertram, whose thematic purpose is to illustrate the vacuity and insensitivity of indolence, has her moment of self-reproach.[1] As for the main characters, every heroine has at least one person of her own sex to set her off; each has two suitors, one good and one bad. As Dr Chapman puts it:

> ... each heroine is furnished with a pendant, rival, or foil; Marianne with Eleanor [*sic*], Elizabeth with Jane, Catherine with Isabella, Fanny with Mary, Emma with Jane; Anne Elliot, whose case does not fit this scheme quite neatly, has two foils to set off her beauty: call her Cordelia, and Miss Elliot assumes the proportions of Goneril, if Mary Musgrove is an inadequate Regan.[2]

Marianne's affections are vied for by Willoughby and by Colonel Brandon – though Elinor's attachment is to but one person, Edward Ferrars; Elizabeth must (briefly) decide between Wickham and Darcy; Catherine is beleaguered by John Thorpe, while she loves Henry Tilney; Fanny is importuned

1. Compare E. M. Forster, *Aspects of the Novel*, London, 1927, pp. 101–105. As he says: 'All the Jane Austen characters are ready for an extended life, for a life which the scheme of her books seldom requires them to lead, and that is why they lead their actual lives so satisfactorily' (pp. 103, 104).
2. R. W. Chapman, *Jane Austen Facts and Problems*, pp. 189, 190.

by Henry Crawford, though her heart belongs to Edmund; Emma considers Frank Churchill, but she is always, rather unconsciously, in love with Mr Knightley; while Anne, though her heart remains true to Captain Wentworth, must endure the attentions of William Walter Elliot. In short, there is a very definite pattern in each of Jane Austen's novels – it is more or less the same pattern all the way through – and the miracle of her genius is that she is able to exhibit so many variations within a relatively narrow and even repeated framework.

Men – as has already been pointed out – play a definitely secondary role: it is through her heroines that she gives exposition to the themes. The men (except Fitzwilliam Darcy, and perhaps Henry Tilney), by complement or contrast, serve, thematically, to deepen and broaden the portraits of the heroines. Furthermore, in each novel there are two important men, the hero and the villain, their respective characters being a comment on one another: the hesitant, inarticulate, pious Edward Ferrars against the eager, talkative rogue, John Willoughby; the brilliant, witty, and perceptive Henry Tilney against the stupid, vulgar, and gross John Thorpe; the proud, austere, high-principled Fitzwilliam Darcy against the open, warm, and disingenuous George Wickham; the cool, priggish, and proper Edmund Bertram against the selfish, clever, and unprincipled Henry Crawford; the strong-willed, correct, and forthright George Knightley against the breezy, hypocritical, and devious Frank Churchill; the plain, upright, simple Captain Frederick Wentworth against the foppish, cruel, and crafty William Walter Elliot.

If we put all the villains together we shall see that one quality they share in common is cleverness, the hypocritical mask of a more or less serious want of principle; the heroes, on the other hand, share in varying degrees a reserve behind which is honesty and strength of feeling. The only two men who do not fall easily within the scope of this generalization are Henry Tilney – though it might be argued that for him wit rather than reserve is the weapon of self-preservation – and

John Thorpe, whose unconcealable stupidity is part and parcel of his boorishness.

In analysing the heroines, heroes, and villains, I shall discuss dramatic irony: it derives its force from the opposition of knowledge to ignorance; the reader (or viewer, in the case of the drama) is aware of what one or more of the characters are not. But the state of ignorance in a character depends upon his predispositions, his human failures of perception, his blinding lack of detachment – and must therefore be considered in this section. On one level, dramatic irony exhibits the contradictions between hope and fulfilment, judgement and actuality, the apparent and the palpable, will and possibility. But on another – and higher – level, it displays the confusion to which the data of sense and instinct give rise: simple ironic reversals no longer yield a 'truer' view of the situation, but offer solace at the end only in that a more comprehensive scrutiny is thus made possible. Dramatic irony, therefore, far from comforting the onlooker with a sense of divine superiority, 'dislocates' the narrow catchwords and easy dogmas which bind our existence to a simple apprehension of the world's possibilities.

I. SENSE AND SENSIBILITY

Elinor and Marianne

Sense and Sensibility is probably Jane Austen's earliest, and certainly her simplest, novel; but like all the rest it can be read on more than one level. On the didactic, or allegorical, level Elinor is the heroine and Marianne her foolish foil; each pretty consistently maintains her representative function throughout, at least until the very end.[1] The novel can thus be read as a satire on the eighteenth-century heroine of sensi-

1. Howells reads it so: '... Elinor is always a person of sense, and Marianne always a person of sensibility.' William Dean Howells, 'Jane Austen's Emma Woodhouse, Marianne Dashwood, and Fanny Price', in his *Heroines of Fiction*, New York and London, 1901, I. p. 71.

bility, a task which Jane Austen performed much more economically and much more pointedly in her juvenile *Love and Freindship*, which plainly and with high comedy carries the premises of the epistolary heroine to their logical conclusions. Nevertheless, from a narrowly moralistic point of view the lesson of *Sense and Sensibility* can be stated as follows: it is wise to behave sensibly, and foolish – even dangerous – to expose oneself to the excesses of sensibility. But on a higher level the book contains the germ of a divided vision: Elinor and Marianne are in fact twin heroines, each embodying a mode of existence which is desirable, but each of which contradicts the other. And the grand irony is that Elinor and Marianne virtually interchange their positions (though there are many modifications along the way): Marianne, it is quite clear, does gradually acquire sense; but it is also true that Elinor becomes increasingly sensitive as the book progresses. So the two elder Dashwood sisters function not as mere allegorical figures but as ironic symbols.

Even at the very beginning of the novel it is clear that both girls have dimensions beyond the terms of the title:

> Elinor ... possessed a strength of understanding, and coolness of judgement, which qualified her, though only nineteen, to be the counsellor of her mother, and enabled her frequently to counteract, to the advantage of them all, that eagerness of mind in Mrs Dashwood which must generally have led to imprudence. She had an excellent heart; – her disposition was affectionate, and her feelings were strong; but she knew how to govern them: it was a knowledge which her mother had yet to learn, and which one of her sisters had resolved never to be taught.
>
> Marianne's abilities were, in many respects, quite equal to Elinor's. She was sensible and clever; but eager in every thing; her sorrows, her joys, could have no moderation. She was generous, amiable, interesting: she was everything but prudent.[1]

It is very possible that the reader of the book will, after absorbing these descriptions, set down Elinor simply as sense and Marianne merely as sensibility; indeed this seems to be

1. *Sense and Sensibility*, p. 6.

the intention of the author, who is seldom averse to misleading her audience. Yet, at least retrospectively, we are led to remark Elinor's affectionate disposition and strong feelings, just as we must know that Marianne's 'eagerness' is but one part (though for many pages the most prominent part) of a nature which possesses intelligence and good sense as well.

The first volume [1] has a symmetrical perfection seldom achieved by Jane Austen or anyone else. So far as the two girls are concerned, there is a clear parallel drawn between the attentions paid them by Edward Ferrars and by John Willoughby. In consonance with Elinor's announced coolness of disposition, her friendship with Edward is conducted on the level of the mind. As she tells Marianne:

> 'I have seen a great deal of him, have studied his sentiments and heard his opinion on subjects of literature and taste; and, upon the whole, I venture to pronounce that his mind is well-informed, his enjoyment of books exceedingly great, his imagination lively, his observation just and correct, and his taste delicate and pure.' [2]

Nor does she seem to suffer when he fails to visit the Dashwoods at Barton Cottage in Devonshire, to which they have removed owing to the odious Mrs John Dashwood.

Marianne, on the other hand, thinks Edward 'spiritless ... tame', and remarks to her mother, '"Mama, the more I know of the world, the more am I convinced that I shall never see a man whom I can really love. I require so much!"' [3] And so she sets the stage for her dramatic encounter with John Willoughby, who rescues her after she has sprained her ankle while walking on the downs near Barton. She does not study his sentiments or hear 'his opinion on subjects of literature and taste', but succumbs to an enchantment which reaches a penultimate climax in his gift of a horse named Queen Mab (which she is persuaded by Elinor to refuse), and which cul-

1. The Chapman edition of the novels preserves the original division into volumes.

2. *Sense and Sensibility*, p. 20.

3. ibid., p. 18.

minates in the imprudent visit to Allenham, the estate which Willoughby will one day inherit. His sudden departure leaves her shattered and sleepless.

By plain contrast, Edward Ferrars's tardy visit to Barton is mild and unexciting:

> ... there was a deficiency of all that a lover ought to look and say on such an occasion. He was confused, seemed scarcely sensible of pleasure in seeing them, looked neither rapturous nor gay, said little but what was forced from him by questions, and distinguished Elinor by no mark of affection.[1]

But Elinor now is no longer satisfied by the conversation which gave her pleasure at Norland – though to be sure he is now even more inarticulate than he was formerly.

> His coldness and reserve mortified her severely; she was vexed and half angry; but resolving to regulate her behaviour to him by the past rather than by the present, she avoided every appearance of resentment or displeasure, and treated him as she thought he ought to be treated from the family connexion.[2]

His departure is just as featureless as his visit, and Elinor's behaviour is outwardly just the opposite of that of Marianne on Willoughby's taking leave; but the elder sister's heart is not untouched, for she thinks of him 'with tenderness, pity, approbation, censure, and doubt'.[3] She has in fact been more aroused than she knows. Her prudent intelligence has caused her to counsel Marianne freely on the dangers of the latter's enthusiastic behaviour with Willoughby; the elder sister's steadiness has given her a control which Marianne mistakes for coldness, and which she cannot in any event emulate. But when the silly Lucy Steele convinces Elinor that Edward has been engaged to her for four years, Elinor is overcome by 'an emotion and distress beyond any thing she had ever felt before. She was mortified, shocked, confounded.'[4]

And so ends the first volume. Marianne has had a first and exciting attachment, which has not yet run its course – so has

1. ibid., p. 87. 2. ibid., p. 89. 3. ibid., p. 105. 4. ibid., p. 135.

Elinor. In a very superficial way the behaviour of the two sisters is strongly contrasted; but in a profounder sense both sisters are stirred by their respective suitors. Marianne has yet to learn sense, but already the sensibility of Elinor has been awakened. The elder sister may still be able to give counsels of sense; but she has already tasted the values of sensibility.

The middle volume is Marianne's story, though the thread which immediately connects it to the first is that of Elinor and Edward, as displayed in the conversations of the elder Dashwood sister with Lucy Steele – at the end of which the former decides with some strength 'that Edward was not only without affection for the person who was to be his wife; but that he had not even the chance of being tolerably happy in marriage. ...' [1] But the scene soon shifts to London, where Marianne hopes to renew her attachment to Willoughby. She is, however, not only disappointed but deeply humiliated, for he both ignores her notes to him and behaves coldly towards her when finally they do meet.

> 'Here is some mistake I am sure – some dreadful mistake. What can be the meaning of it? Tell me, Willoughby; for heaven's sake tell me, what is the matter?' [2]

But he only murmurs a feeble formality and turns away. Her feverish access of grief reaches its climax the next day, however, when she receives the letter from Willoughby in which he calmly denies that his intentions have ever been serious. Elinor tries to console her sister, but the latter remains inconsolable:

> 'Oh! how easy for those who have no sorrow of their own to talk of exertion! Happy, happy Elinor, *you* cannot have an idea of what I suffer.' [3]

And here, of course, Marianne is uttering an unconscious irony – for Elinor's distress has been longer in duration, more profound in scope, and much less likely to be relieved – Edward is engaged to be married; Willoughby, at least, is not.

1. *Sense and Sensibility*, p. 151. 2. ibid., p. 177. 3. ibid., p. 185.

But almost immediately the news of Willoughby's engagement to Miss Sophia Grey is revealed to Marianne, whose experience now exactly parallels Elinor's. Again she undergoes sleepless grief, again she is beyond comfort; nor does she derive much satisfaction from Colonel Brandon's testimony that Willoughby has seduced Eliza – that in fact the two men have duelled over the matter.

Now the focus shifts to the Ferrars family, whose charms are nil, Mrs Ferrars's impoliteness being only less galling to Elinor than Edward's continued inarticulateness. But in this volume the emphasis has fallen upon Marianne. We cannot help censuring the excesses to which she has laid herself open – or at least we are forced to wish that she could moderate her emotional responses. But we cannot stop loving her, however unsensibly she behaves. Marianne is no Isabella Thorpe, no mere cruel parody of a Richardson heroine; she is a fully developed human being whose hopes and despairs we sympathize with. We love her partly because of her sensibility, which we learn from Jane Austen both to treasure and condemn.

In the final – and most imperfect – volume Elinor and Marianne become increasingly like each other, a process which makes both of them more rounded and complete people. The first sign of Marianne's change comes at the beginning, when she learns that Edward and Lucy are engaged, and that Elinor has known for four months, but has been able to maintain an outward composure.

> Marianne was quite subdued.
>
> 'Oh! Elinor,' she cried, 'you have made me hate myself for ever. – How barbarous have I been to you! – you, who have been my only comfort, who have borne with me in all my misery, who have seemed to be only suffering for me! – Is this my gratitude! – Is this the only return I can make you? – Because your merit cries out upon myself, I have been trying to do it away.' [1]

So does Marianne begin to learn something of her sister's

1. ibid., p. 264.

fortitude in facing life; and she finally is able to recover from the Willoughby affair. Her illness leads her to reflect on the impetuosity of her behaviour, and she resolves that in the future '"my feelings shall be governed and my temper improved"'.[1] She so governs Brandon's proposal of marriage. Elinor, on the other hand, as the plot untwists the difficulties which lie between her and Edward Ferrars, moves towards a glorious fulfilment of her deepest wishes: 'she was oppressed, she was overcome by her own felicity; – and happily disposed as is the human mind to be easily familiarized with any change for the better, it required several hours to give sedateness to her spirits, or any degree of tranquillity to her heart.'[2]

At the very end of the book, the author intrudes enough to write:

> Marianne Dashwood was born to an extraordinary fate. She was born to discover the falsehood of her own opinions, and to counteract, by her conduct, her most favourite maxims. She was born to overcome an affection formed so late in life as at seventeen, and with no sentiment superior to strong esteem and lively friendship, voluntarily to give her hand to another! – and *that* other, a man who had suffered no less than herself under the event of a former attachment, whom, two years before, she had considered too old to be married, – and who still sought the constitutional safeguard of a flannel waistcoat![3]

But her sister was born to no less an extraordinary fate, the fate of a girl whose first and only attachment was to lead to the most romantic and happy of marriages. And so we are forced to ask ourselves which mode Jane Austen chooses. Does sense solve every problem, does sense deal adequately with life? Elinor, the apotheosis of sense, shows us that it does not: she is not saved the miseries of despair, though outwardly she is able to bear them with greater composure than her sister; she does not make a *mariage de convenance*, but a marriage of love to a far from wealthy clergyman. Marianne, on the other hand, over-compensates for her early want of

1. *Sense and Sensibility*, p. 347. 2. ibid., p. 363. 3. ibid., p. 378.

sense by making a perhaps too eminently sensible marriage. And the 'lesson' of the book is that neither mode is adequate, each contradicts the other – and there is no happy medium.

Edward Ferrars and John Willoughby

The interaction between the future husband of Elinor Dashwood and the man who trifles with Marianne's affections offers a sharp contrast which is, in turn, meant to draw a parallel between the two sisters themselves. Functionally, they succeed; but by themselves they are certainly the least interesting pair to be found in the Jane Austen canon – Edward because he is too broadly outlined; Willoughby because he is too rudely yanked about by his author for the purpose of the plot to be a credible human being.

Edward Ferrars was not recommended ... by any peculiar graces of person or address. He was not handsome, and his manners required intimacy to make them pleasing. He was too diffident to do justice to himself; but when his natural shyness was overcome, his behaviour gave every indication of an open affectionate heart. His understanding was good, and his education had given it solid improvement. But he was neither fitted by abilities nor disposition to answer the wishes of his mother and sister, who longed to see him distinguished – as – they hardly knew what. ... All his wishes centered in domestic comfort and the quiet of private life. Fortunately he had a younger brother who was more promising.[1]

Who can blame Marianne for finding him 'spiritless' and 'tame' ? Several of Jane Austen's fictional people start off thus, but then surprise us by acquiring a greater interest as the book unfolds. Catherine Morland is an example – as is even the somewhat stuffy Edmund Bertram, whose attachment to Miss Crawford discloses a real human warmth. Edward, on the other hand, becomes increasingly uninteresting: his reserve, when he visits the Dashwoods at Barton, is positively gauche; and the one exciting deviation in his life (the engagement to Lucy Steele) has nearly all taken place before the book begins,

1. ibid., pp. 15, 16.

so that it is impossible to explore that relationship except in its final and least interesting stages.

Even his proposal of marriage is not only hesitant but (very possibly) phlegmatic:

> His errand at Barton, in fact, was a simple one. It was only to ask Elinor to marry him; – and considering that he was not altogether inexperienced in such a question, it might be strange that he should feel so uncomfortable in the present case as he really did, so much in need of encouragement and fresh air.
>
> How soon he had walked himself into the proper resolution, however, how soon an opportunity of exercising it occurred, in what manner he expressed himself, and how he was received need not be particularly told. This only need be said; – that when they all sat down to table at four o'clock, about three hours after his arrival, he had secured his lady. . . .[1]

John Willoughby, on the other hand, is a regular villain, a less interesting, because less complete, version of Richardson's Lovelace, whom he resembles in his carefree gaiety, insensitive wit, his propensity to seduction, and in his final, pious repentance.[2]

He appears first in the romantic role of rescuer. To the quiet, retired existence at Barton he brings a sparkle and an interest which Colonel Brandon, with his flannel waistcoats, has never been able to provide. And his romance with Marianne proceeds quickly. She, who has declared herself unable to stomach second attachments, has been completely captivated and jumps at the chance to go to London, where, quite contrary to her expectations, he ignores her completely until finally he is constrained to speak, after failing to reply to several of her letters and after behaving with arrant rudeness to her at a party.

1. *Sense and Sensibility*, p. 361.

2. Compare Léonie Villard: 'Willoughby, the attractive "black sheep" . . . is a blurred and softened reproduction of Lovelace, the unscrupulous lover, the libertine and seducer, created by Richardson.' *Jane Austen: a French Appreciation*, p. 243.

MY DEAR MADAM,

I have just had the honour of receiving your letter, for which I beg to return my sincere acknowledgements. I am much concerned to find there was any thing in my behaviour last night that did not meet your approbation; and though I am quite at a loss to discover in what point I could be so unfortunate as to offend you, I entreat your forgiveness of what I can assure you to have been perfectly unintentional. I shall never reflect on my former acquaintance with your family in Devonshire without the most grateful pleasure, and flatter myself it will not be broken by any mistake or misapprehension of my actions. My esteem for your whole family is very sincere; but if I have been so unfortunate as to give rise to a belief of more than I felt, or meant to express, I shall reproach myself for not having been more guarded in my professions of that esteem. That I should ever have meant more you will allow to be impossible, when you understand that my affections have been long engaged elsewhere, and it will not be many weeks, I believe, before this engagement is fulfilled. It is with great regret that I obey your commands of returning the letters, with which I have been honoured from you, and the lock of hair, which you so obligingly bestowed on me.[1]

This letter is a masterpiece of nastiness, but nastiness is not the worst of John Willoughby, whose seduction of the illegitimate little Eliza is soon disclosed. Appropriately enough, all this latter has happened off-stage; otherwise, the comic tone of the novel would have been seriously impaired. But – and this is quite inappropriate to the book – there comes in the final pages Willoughby's confession and repentance, and Elinor's forgiveness of him. Thinking that Marianne is on her death-bed, he comes to Cleveland, where with great humility he expatiates upon his realization of his own rascality. He says to Elinor:

'Tell her of my misery and my penitence – tell her that my heart was never inconstant to her, and if you will, that at this moment she is dearer to me than ever.' [2]

Elinor forgives him – but we can hardly forgive Jane Austen.

1. *Sense and Sensibility*, p. 183. 2. ibid., p. 330.

2. NORTHANGER ABBEY

Catherine Morland

As a satire of the Gothic horror tale, *Northanger Abbey* contains all the ingredients of this genre except the hero and heroine, who are deliberately normalized, partly for the purpose of heightening the ridicule. Like all parodies the book exhibits two sets of values: one is satirized, the other (by implication) is shown to be 'truer'. Here, the illusions of Gothic sentimentality are contrasted to the less flashy but more durable values of good sense; the Gothic world is one of fancy, the world as apprehended by good sense is 'real'. But the book goes somewhat beyond these limits – it goes beyond to explore the limitations of good sense itself. And Jane Austen shows us that though we must reject the Gothic world as inadequate and false, we cannot altogether apprehend the real world by good sense alone. Good sense, ironically, is limited too.

In sketching Catherine Morland's background, appearance, and disposition, her author manages to suggest both the typical Gothic heroine and, in Catherine herself, the inverse: [1]

> [Catherine] had a thin awkward figure, a sallow skin without colour, dark lank hair, and strong features; – so much for her person; – and not less unpropitious for heroism seemed her mind. She was fond of all boys' plays, and greatly preferred cricket not merely to dolls, but to the more heroic enjoyments of infancy, nursing a dormouse, feeding a canary-bird, or watering a rose-bush. ... Such were her propensities – her abilities were quite as extraordinary. She never could learn or understand any thing before she was taught; and sometimes not even then, for she was often inattentive, and occasionally stupid. ... What a strange, unaccountable character! [2]

So she was at the age of ten, but when we find her, on the brink of a six weeks' visit to Bath, she has grown:

> ... her heart was affectionate, her disposition cheerful and open, without conceit or affectation of any kind – her manners just re-

1. Professor Mudrick makes this point, op. cit., p. 42.
2. *Northanger Abbey*, pp. 13, 14.

moved from the awkwardness and shyness of a girl; her person pleasing, and, when in good looks, pretty – and her mind about as ignorant and uninformed as the female mind at seventeen usually is.[1]

Her experiences, on first arriving at Bath, are a combination of what might be expected from the Gothic heroine, and the very reverse. The Allens, whose guest she is, are an ordinary, unexciting Wiltshire couple; her first visit to the Upper Rooms produces ennui rather than rapture; the young man she meets is no silent, olive-faced seducer from Southern Europe, but a talkative, sardonic clergyman from Gloucestershire named Henry Tilney, whose father is a general, and who lectures Catherine on the inadequacies of young ladies as letter-writers and other things. On the other hand, she meets Isabella Thorpe, who begins as a regular Gothic confidante (though she ends as an Austenian villain), who induces Catherine to read *The Mysteries of Udolpho* and will give her a list of 'horrid' books to read; she encounters the flashy and dishonest John Thorpe who endeavours to take her to Blaize Castle.

But far more important than her Gothic indoctrination at Bath is her own emergence as a human being – though she is not to be cured of the Gothic infection until her experience at Northanger Abbey, in the second volume. At once she is drawn to Isabella Thorpe, whose conversation is expert on such subjects as:

... dress, balls, flirtations, and quizzes. ... These powers received due admiration from Catherine, to whom they were entirely new; and the respect which they naturally inspired might have been too great for familiarity, had not the easy gaiety of Miss Thorpe's manners, and her frequent expressions of delight on this acquaintance with her, softened down every feeling of awe, and left nothing but tender affection.[2]

Youth and a natural credulousness have led her to make this unquestioning friendship with Isabella; but John Thorpe affects

1. ibid., p. 18. 2. ibid., pp. 33, 34.

her differently even at the beginning of their acquaintance. He is stout, loud, impudent, boastful, insensitive, and dishonest – and:

> Little as Catherine was in the habit of judging for herself, and unfixed as were her general notions of what men ought to be, she could not entirely repress a doubt, while she bore with the effusions of his endless conceit, of his being altogether agreeable.[1]

Indeed she is soon forced to make a conscious and quite firm judgement against him, when he lies to her in order to persuade her to ride to Blaize Castle with him. Made to think for herself on this occasion, and increasingly allied with the sensible Tilney family, she is gradually able to see Isabella with greater objectivity. When the latter claims that Miss Tilney has supplanted her in Catherine's heart

> Catherine thought this reproach equally strange and unkind. Was it the part of a friend thus to expose her feelings to the notice of others? Isabella appeared to her ungenerous and selfish, regardless of every thing but her own gratification.[2]

But Catherine is forced to suspend, or soften, her judgement of Isabella when the latter becomes engaged to Catherine's brother James. Meanwhile, Catherine's increased intimacy with the Tilneys (and a mistaken impression on the general's part as to her wealth) evokes an invitation to Northanger Abbey, the setting of the major part of the second volume.

Here, with beautifully comic anti-climax, Jane Austen traces Catherine's Gothic adventures. Having expected 'long damp passages . . . narrow cells and [a] ruined chapel . . . some awful memorials of an injured and ill-fated nun', she finds 'lodges of a modern appearance . . . a smooth, level road of fine gravel, without obstacle, alarm or solemnity of any kind. . . .'[3] In her bedroom, which is far from horrifying in most respects, she finds a mysterious chest – it contains a cotton counterpane; she later spies another chest which frightens her out of a full night's sleep – this contains an inventory of linen.

1 *Northanger Abbey*, p. 66. 2. ibid., p. 98. 3. ibid., pp. 141, 161.

She steals to the room where Mrs Tilney died, expected to see evidence that the lady is still alive and cruelly imprisoned – but finds instead a neat, well-lighted, empty bedroom. Henry Tilney finally convinces her that his mother died quite normally, of a ' "bilious fever" '. And so at last Catherine is purged of her Gothic illusions.

Charming as were all Mrs Radcliffe's works and charming even as were the works of all her imitators, it was not in them perhaps that human nature, at least in the midland counties of England, was to be looked for. Of the Alps and Pyrenees, with their pine forests and their vices, they might give a faithful delineation. . . . But in the central part of England there was surely some security for the existence even of a wife not beloved, in the laws of the land, and the manners of the age. Murder was not tolerated, servants were not slaves, and neither poison nor sleeping potions to be procured, like rhubarb, from every druggist.[1]

But, side by side with her awakening from the Gothic dream, is her much more important emergence as a human being of good sense – and the gradual realization of the limitations of even that quality. It is chiefly through her relationship with Isabella and with John Thorpe that she is thus educated.

We have already seen that at first Catherine is disposed to like Isabella, to accept her unquestioningly as a friend, largely because of the older girl's high spirits. This acceptance is questioned briefly when Isabella expresses some jealousy about the relationship of Catherine to Miss Tilney – but modified when James Morland and Isabella become engaged. Catherine is shocked when Captain Tilney (Henry's older brother) and Isabella commence a flirtation; but she is too good-heartedly naïve to be suspicious:

It seemed to her that Captain Tilney was falling in love with Isabella, and Isabella unconsciously encouraging him; unconsciously it must be, for Isabella's attachment to James was as certain and well acknowledged as her engagement. To doubt her truth or good intentions was impossible; and yet, during the whole of their conversation her manner had been odd.[2]

1. ibid., p. 200. 2. ibid., p. 148.

Catherine grows resentful, however, of Isabella's insensitivity, but is rather surprised, when she hears that Captain Tilney and Isabella have become engaged (James having been thrown off), that she does not much regret the loss of Isabella's friendship.

'To say the truth, though I am hurt and grieved, that I cannot still love her, that I am never to hear from her, perhaps never to see her again, I do not feel so very, very much afflicted as one would have thought.' [1]

But this is not the end of her relationship to Isabella, who coolly writes that she loves James after all, and urges Catherine to intervene with her brother on their behalf.

Such a strain of shallow artifice could not impose even upon Catherine. Its inconsistencies, contradictions, and falsehood, struck her from the very first. She was ashamed of Isabella, and ashamed of having ever loved her. Her professions of attachment were now as disgusting as her excuses were empty, and her demands impudent. 'Write to James on her behalf! – No, James should never hear Isabella's name mentioned by her again.' [2]

If the relationship to the Thorpes shows Catherine the value of common sense in evaluating life's difficulties, the relationship to the Tilneys (except the Gothic trimmings) discloses the limits of this virtue. She meets and is attracted to, though she is rather baffled by, Henry Tilney; she becomes the friend of Eleanor; she is treated with affectionate kindness by the rather terrifying General Tilney – and then suddenly she is dismissed without explanation, on the General's return from a short journey to London. She is stunned, almost overcome with grief, and returns home to Wiltshire in deep humiliation; there she meets with the unfailing kindness and sympathy of her family, and is induced to walk to the Allens', who live near by.

As they walked home again, Mrs Morland endeavoured to impress on her daughter's mind the happiness of having such steady well-wishers as Mr and Mrs Allen, and the very little consideration

1. *Northanger Abbey*, p. 207. 2. ibid., p. 218.

which the neglect or unkindness of slight acquaintance like the Tilneys ought to have with her, while she could preserve the good opinion and affection of her earliest friends. There was a great deal of good sense in all this; but there are some situations of the human mind in which good sense has very little power; and Catherine's feelings contradicted almost every position her mother advanced.[1]

And so, momentarily, Catherine sees the unresolvable irony between the strong heart and the clear mind: she has been educated by her experiences at Bath and at the Tilneys' to the superior value of common sense. Now, almost before she has been able to absorb the lesson, she learns that good sense cannot deal with the crisis that has forced her sudden expulsion. But the happy dénouement is less than ten pages away, the heroine in the arms of her beloved Henry; and Jane Austen writes, sardonically: 'I leave it to be settled by whomever it may concern: whether the tendency of this work be altogether to recommend parental tyranny, or reward filial disobedience.'[2]

Compared to Jane Austen's later heroines Catherine Morland is somewhat thin. Professor Mudrick remarks: 'She is too simple and too slight, too narrowly a symbol of the author's rejection of romantic nonsense, to assert the claim of personal feeling and value beyond mere function.'[3] Howells writes of her:

> Catherine Morland is a goose, but a very engaging goose, and a goose you must respect for her sincerity, her high principles, her generous trust of others, and her patience under trials that would be too great for much stronger heads ... and in spite of her romantic folly she has so much good heart that it serves her in place of good sense.[4]

It seems to me that both these critics rather miss the point about Catherine: her inadequacies as a heroine, such as they are, exist because Jane Austen tries to do too much with her – to establish her both as a gooselike parody of the

1. ibid., p. 239.
2. ibid., p. 252.
3. Mudrick, op. cit., p. 53.
4. Howells, op. cit., I, p. 58.

sentimental-Gothic heroine, and to advance claims for her as a human being who would learn good sense, and learn even to go beyond it. To be sure, irony is not central to the story; *Northanger Abbey*'s delight lies principally in the amusing parody which it presents. But the indication that there is more on earth than mere common sense gives the book an ironic dimension of enduring value.

Henry Tilney and John Thorpe

Henry Tilney is the only one of Jane Austen's heroes who shares her ironic viewpoint, the only one who ever threatens the primacy of a heroine. But this must be, for in *Northanger Abbey* Jane Austen chooses a heroine who is marvellously credulous and naïve – but who, miraculously, wins our affection and even admiration, as Harriet Smith (for instance) does not. John Thorpe contrasts sharply with Henry Tilney in being gross where the latter is refined, stupid rather than brilliant, boorish rather than elegant; Thorpe appears very little, is dismissed early, and is, altogether, the least interesting of his author's villains – partly, perhaps, because the real villain of the piece (though a rather nice one) consists of Catherine's Gothic illusions.

Henry Tilney first appears – as is appropriate to a burlesque of the novel of terror – on a *decrescendo*. Instead of encountering the heroine mysteriously or in a situation of great danger, he is introduced to her by the Master of Ceremonies of the Lower Rooms at Bath. After playfully inquiring as to her activities in Bath, he engages her on the subject of female letter-writing. He observes:

> 'As far as I have had the opportunity of judging, it appears to me that the usual style of letter-writing among women is faultless, except in three particulars.'
>
> 'And what are they?'
>
> 'A general deficiency of subject, a total inattention to stops, and a very frequent ignorance of grammar.' [1]

1. *Northanger Abbey*, p. 27.

His function throughout the novel is not only to provide by his cleverness, his wit, and his *savoir-vivre* a sharp contrast to the 'goosish' heroine, but to take over as leading proponent of Jane Austen's viewpoint, whenever circumstances require.

Naturally, the relationship between Henry and Catherine deepens, the latter usually bewildered by his bursts of cleverness. When, finally, she is invited to visit Northanger Abbey, he engagingly prepares her for the terrors of the place. '"... are you prepared to encounter all the horrors that a building such as 'what one reads about' may produce? – Have you a stout heart? – Nerves fit for sliding panels and tapestry?"' [1] But of course it does not live up to her Gothic expectations. All in all, he adds up to a thoroughly attractive young man, quite exceeding his functional responsibilities. R. W. Chapman, discussing the heroes of Jane Austen's novels, says: '... I retain a sneaking preference for Henry Tilney: for no better reason, perhaps, than that I find in him a resemblance to my youthful priggishness. But he has more wit than any of her young men except Henry Crawford.' [2]

John Thorpe is not much worse than rude, vain, selfish, stupid, boastful, and dishonest. He does not seduce anyone, like John Willoughby; defame anyone, like George Wickham; coolly run off with a married woman, like Henry Crawford; deceive anyone (except General Tilney), like Frank Churchill; or insolently ignore the claims of an indigent widow, like Mr Elliot. John Thorpe is simply:

> ... a stout young man of middling height, who, with a plain face and ungraceful form, seemed fearful of being too handsome unless he wore the dress of a groom, and too much like a gentleman unless he were easy where he ought to be civil, and impudent where he might be allowed to be easy.[3]

He does not even deceive Catherine Morland very long; before he lies to her about the Tilneys, she is put off by his endless chatter of the famous parties in his Oxford rooms, races,

1. ibid., pp. 157, 158. 2. *Jane Austen Facts and Problems*, p. 201.
3. *Northanger Abbey*, p. 45.

shooting-parties, fox-hunting – in all of which he claims to have played a leading and heroic role.

But his worst defection lies in his behaviour when he desires that Catherine accompany him to Bristol, where (with Isabella Thorpe and James Morland) they will visit Blaize Castle. She tells him that she is already engaged to go walking with the Tilneys; he replies that the latter have already set out in a carriage and therefore will not go walking that day. So Catherine acquiesces; but, *en route*, catches sight of the Tilneys on foot. Thorpe has lied – but will not stop, despite Catherine's strong entreaties. Catherine is furious; her eyes are now thoroughly opened to his character – and henceforth he fades out of the picture very fast, leaving the heroine to battle only her own illusions. The reader is left with the feeling that John Thorpe is the least necessary of Jane Austen's villains, and is perhaps the least interesting both to his author and to his audience.

As in Jane Austen's other novels, hero and villain in *Northanger Abbey* function principally to sharpen and define the position, the personality, and the development of the heroine. John Thorpe is a crude Lovelace, whose defects Catherine sees almost at once – despite the overlay of Gothic fantasy in her mind; Henry Tilney is the agent of Catherine's gradual unillusionment, but as an attractive young man to whom she responds ardently, he unknowingly leads her to the edge of common sense – and beyond.

3. PRIDE AND PREJUDICE

Elizabeth Bennet

At first glance, perhaps, the two elder Bennet sisters may seem to vie with each other for primacy in *Pride and Prejudice*; but Elizabeth is definitely the heroine: not only does she explicitly represent one of the words of the title of the story; she also quite thoroughly dominates the action – and, by comparison, Jane is a shadowy accessory. The relationship of Miss Bennet to Bingley, which parallels that of Elizabeth and Darcy, is treated much less fully, partly because it is much simpler, but partly because it is intended to be a comment on that of her younger sister and the proud man from Derbyshire. Yet Jane throughout the book has the unqualified approbation of Elizabeth, author, and reader – though we may, with Elizabeth, wish to speak to her with the following affectionate mock-exasperation:

> 'My dear Jane! ... you are too good. Your sweetness and disinterestedness are really angelic; I do not know what to say to you. I feel as if I had never done you justice, or loved you as you deserve.' [1]

Indeed it is because of – not despite – her perfection that we must reject Jane as the heroine: the author's concern is with the complexity, the interrelationship, of good and bad – the mixture which cannot be unmixed. Jane is a simple character, but ' "intricate characters are the *most* amusing" ',[2] and Jane, like Bingley, is not intricate: she is heroic but minor – she is not a heroine. 'I must confess,' writes Jane Austen of Elizabeth Bennet, 'that I think her as delightful a creature as ever appeared in print, and how I shall be able to tolerate those who do not like *her* at least I do not know.' [3]

To say that Darcy is proud and Elizabeth prejudiced is to tell but half the story. Pride and prejudice are faults; but they are also the necessary defects of desirable merits: self-respect and intelligence. Moreover, the novel makes clear the fact that Darcy's pride leads to prejudice and Elizabeth's prejudice stems from a pride in her own perceptions. So the ironic theme of the book might be said to centre on the dangers of intellectual complexity. Jane Bennet and Bingley are never exposed to these dangers; they are not sufficiently profound. But the hero and the heroine, because of their deep percipience, are, ironically, subject to failures of perception. Elizabeth has good reason to credit herself with the ability to discern people and situations extraordinarily well: she understands her family

1. *Pride and Prejudice*, pp. 134, 135.
2. ibid., p. 42.
3. *Letters*, II, p. 297 (to Cassandra Austen, 29 January 1813).

perfectly, knows William Collins from the first letter he writes, comprehends the merits and deficiencies of the Bingleys almost at once, appreciates Lady Catherine de Bourgh at first meeting. Her failures are with 'intricate' people who moreover stand in a relationship of great intimacy to her: Charlotte Lucas, George Wickham, Fitzwilliam Darcy. And the book is given an added dimension because it shows that intimacy blurs perceptions: intelligence fails if there is insufficient distance between mind and object.

Charlotte Lucas is 'a sensible, intelligent young woman, about twenty-seven ... Elizabeth's intimate friend'.[1] But we very soon know that in an important respect she differs from Elizabeth – though Elizabeth herself does not know this fact. When, very early in the first volume, they discuss the possibility of an attachment between Jane and Bingley, Charlotte says Jane should make some efforts in this direction; but Elizabeth reminds her friend that Miss Bennet hardly knows him. This, however, does not deter Charlotte:

> 'I wish Jane success with all my heart; and if she were married to him tomorrow, I should think she had as good a chance of happiness, as if she were to be studying his character for a twelvemonth. Happiness in marriage is entirely a matter of chance. If the dispositions of the parties are ever so well known to each other, or ever so similar before-hand, it does not advance their felicity in the least. They always continue to grow sufficiently unlike afterwards to have their share of vexation; and it is better to know as little as possible of the defects of the person with whom you are to pass your life.'[2]

But Elizabeth does not believe this statement:

> 'You make me laugh, Charlotte; but it is not sound. You know it is not sound, and that you would never act in this way yourself.'[3]

Why does she refuse to believe Charlotte (who will soon demonstrate quite shockingly that she means every word she

1. *Pride and Prejudice*, p. 18. 2. ibid., p. 23. 3. ibid., p. 23.

says on the subject of marriage)? It is because a natural kindness and affection have blinded Elizabeth to the demerits of her friend; it is because, in the nature of things, involvement (which is so necessary and desirable, in Austenian terms) carries with it the inevitable consequence of obscuring the marvellous clarity and depth of understanding so necessary to success in personal association.

There is no evidence that Charlotte misunderstands William Collins, but there is much to show that Elizabeth does comprehend him perfectly. '"Can he be a sensible man, sir?"'[1] she asks her father rhetorically after hearing the orotund phrases of the clergyman's letter. Nor is she wrong. At the Netherfield Ball, after dancing with him twice, 'the moment of her release from him was exstacy',[2] but she derives some consolation in discussing his demerits with Charlotte. The next morning he proposes marriage to Elizabeth ('"And now nothing remains for me but to assure you in the most animated language of the violence of my affection"'),[3] and of course she refuses him summarily. Then she is flabbergasted to learn that Charlotte has accepted Mr Collins's subsequent proposal of marriage to her.

> She had always felt that Charlotte's opinion of matrimony was not exactly like her own, but she could not have supposed it possible that when called into action, she would have sacrificed every better feeling to worldly advantage. Charlotte the wife of Mr Collins was a most humiliating picture![4]

And now, for the first time, she begins to see Charlotte as she really is: and 'felt persuaded that no real confidence could ever subsist between them again'.[5] Elizabeth has learned something from this experience, as is demonstrated in her conversation with Jane not long afterwards:

> 'Do not be afraid of my running into any excess, of my encroaching on your privilege of universal good will. You need not. There

1. ibid., p. 64. 2. ibid., p. 90. 3. ibid., p. 106.
4. ibid., p. 125. 5. ibid., p. 128.

are few people whom I really love, and still fewer of whom I think well. The more I see of the world, the more am I dissatisfied with it; and every day confirms my belief of the inconsistency of all human characters, and of the little dependence that can be placed on the appearance of either merit or sense. I have met with two instances lately; one I will not mention [it is Bingley's 'want of proper resolution']; the other is Charlotte's marriage. It is unaccountable! In every view it is unaccountable!'[1]

Elizabeth does not give Darcy a chance – or rather she does not give herself a chance to know how she really feels about him. The famous first encounter is comically disastrous; it occurs at the assembly where Darcy says to Bingley of Elizabeth, who is sitting down: ' "She is tolerable; but not handsome enough to tempt *me*; and I am in no humour at present to give consequence to young ladies who are slighted by other men." ' And as a natural result, 'Elizabeth remained with no very cordial feelings towards him.'[2]

But at Netherfield, where she has gone to nurse the ailing Jane, Elizabeth makes her extraordinary and attractive personality felt – so strongly that Mrs Hurst and Miss Bingley take an immediate dislike to her; so strongly that she finds Darcy staring at her.

She hardly knew how to suppose that she could be an object of admiration to so great a man; and yet that he should look at her because he disliked her, was still more strange. She could only imagine however at last, that she drew his notice because there was a something about her more wrong and reprehensible, according to his ideas of right, than in any other person present. The supposition did not pain her. She liked him too little to care for his approbation.[3]

However, when she refuses to dance with him and says, ' "despise me if you dare," ' he replies in unmistakable accents, ' "Indeed I do not dare." '[4]

With the insult of the Ball fresh in her mind, she does not

1. *Pride and Prejudice*, p. 135. 2. ibid., p. 12.
3. ibid., p. 51. 4. ibid., p. 52.

like him; she is even willing to overweigh the negative evidence, which now presents itself first from Darcy himself, then from the plausible and attractive Wickham. In the conversation at Netherfield, during which Elizabeth makes her well-known remark, that ' "I hope I never ridicule what is wise and good," ' she finds from Darcy that ' "My good opinion once lost is lost for ever" ' [1] – a chilling comment which she acknowledges to be a defect, but not a laughable one.

Then she meets Wickham and, finding him charming, very easily believes his allegations that Darcy has behaved abominably, that the latter has cast the young lieutenant from a promised living in the church, that in fact both Darcy and his sister suffer from very excessive pride. Elizabeth is vexed and even angry when Wickham fails to appear at the Netherfield Ball, again not trying to suppose that there may be something to be said on Darcy's side. Even so, there are signs that she willy-nilly succumbs to his charms – in the pertness of her conversation while they are dancing:

'It is *your* turn to say something now, Mr Darcy. – *I* talked about the dance, and *you* ought to make some kind of remark on the size of the room, or the number of couples.'

He smiled, and assured her that whatever she wished him to say should be said.

'Very well. – That reply will do for the present. – Perhaps by and bye I may observe that private balls are much pleasanter than public ones. – But *now* we may be silent.'

'Do you talk by rule then, while you are dancing?'

'Sometimes. One must speak a little, you know. It would look odd to be entirely silent for half an hour together, and yet for the advantage of *some*, conversation ought to be so arranged as that they may have the trouble of saying as little as possible.'

'Are you consulting your own feelings in the present case, or do you imagine that you are gratifying mine?'

'Both,' replied Elizabeth archly; 'for I have always seen a great similarity in the turn of our minds. – We are each of an unsocial, taciturn disposition, unwilling to speak, unless we expect to say

1. *Pride and Prejudice*, pp. 57, 58.

something that will amaze the whole room, and be handed down to posterity with all the éclat of a proverb.' [1]

However, when she questions him about Wickham, he keeps silent – nor can she understand him, as she readily admits before their dance is finished. It is an artful irony of Jane Austen's that Miss Bingley immediately thereafter tells her that Wickham is entirely in the wrong, and Darcy in the right, in the breach between the two men. Elizabeth disbelieves her for two reasons: first, because she has correctly sized Miss Bingley up as an entirely unreliable source of information; and second, perhaps, because she *wants* to dislike Darcy in order to avoid any entanglement which will cost her her freedom. Nevertheless, she feels mortified when she realizes that Darcy is overhearing Mrs Bennet boast that Jane and Bingley will soon be engaged.

In the second volume, the relationship of Darcy and Elizabeth is resumed in Kent, at Rosings, and at Hunsford, the parsonage to which William Collins has taken his new wife. Everything is unpropitious, so far as Elizabeth herself is concerned: she has agreed to visit Charlotte only because of the memory of their close friendship – 'all the comfort of intimacy was over.' [2] Mr Collins is just as senseless as ever; Miss de Bourgh is ' "sickly and cross. – Yes, she will do for him [Darcy] very well. She will make him a very proper wife" '; [3] and Lady Catherine is quite as insufferable as Wickham has promised. Among all these displeasing people comes Darcy, who adds to her annoyance by looking confused when she asks whether he has seen Jane in London (for she suspects that he has warned Bingley off her); and, despite his calls at the parsonage and their 'chance' encounters in Rosings Park, her prejudice against him increases, for she finds apparent corroboration of her suspicions in the conversation with Colonel Fitzwilliam, during which he recounts the fact that Darcy has told him of saving an intimate friend recently from a very imprudent marriage.

And so she is bowled over when Darcy tells her he loves her:

1. *Pride and Prejudice*, p. 91. 2. ibid., p. 146. 3. ibid., p. 158.

'In vain have I struggled. It will not do. My feelings will not be repressed. You must allow me to tell you how ardently I admire and love you.' [1]

But she is more than astonished: she is gradually angered by the tone and implication of his remarks:

His sense of her inferiority – of its being a degradation – of the family obstacles which judgement had always opposed to inclination, were dwelt on with a warmth which seemed due to the consequence he was wounding, but was very unlikely to recommend his suit.[2]

So – and not without recrimination for ' "ruining, perhaps for ever, the happiness of a most beloved sister" ' and for his ill-treatment of Wickham – she refuses and dismisses the proud Mr Fitzwilliam Darcy.

But this is not the end: indeed it is only the beginning of Elizabeth's very gradually successful efforts to know herself thoroughly. The next day she is handed Darcy's justly famous letter, written in proud tones and offering some new light not only on the Jane-Bingley business but upon the supposed unfairness to Wickham's claims. As to the first, Darcy says he thought Jane seemed not much attracted to Bingley, whereas Bingley was strongly attached to Jane; and furthermore, Darcy acknowledges an objection to Miss Bennet's family – two considerations which led him both to conceal from Bingley the fact of Jane's presence in London and to persuade his friend that she did not feel much affection for him. As for Wickham, the young Meryton militiaman resigned all claim to a living, in return for which Darcy gave him £3000 to study law. Three years later, the incumbent of the living, the claim to which Wickham had resigned, died; and Wickham, having lived a dissipated and extravagant life in London, sought it. Darcy refused, and Wickham abused him violently; but, more than that, sought Georgiana Darcy out, and persuaded her to elope with him – though the plot was prevented.

Elizabeth reads the letter with great astonishment and – at first – with little comprehension. She is, however, even more

1. ibid., p. 189. 2. ibid., p. 189.

completely stunned by the account of Wickham, and her first impression is to disbelieve Darcy on that score too. But then, in reflecting on Wickham's behaviour at Meryton (especially with regard to his sudden betrothal to the rich Miss King), she is inclined to think it very probable that Darcy is telling the truth after all.

> She grew absolutely ashamed of herself. – Of neither Darcy nor Wickham could she think, without feeling that she had been blind, partial, prejudiced, absurd.
>
> 'How despicably have I acted!' she cried. – 'I, who have prided myself on my discernment! – I, who have valued myself on my abilities! who have often disdained the generous candour of my sister, and gratified my vanity, in useless or blameable distrust. – How humiliating is this discovery! – Yet, how just a humiliation! – Had I been in love, I could not have been more wretchedly blind.' [1]

In this dramatic moment of self-revelation she has the honesty to see that there may be some justice in what Darcy has said about Jane, for 'she felt that Jane's feelings, though fervent, were little displayed, and that there was a constant complacency in her air and manner, not often united with great sensibility'. [2] She has learned much from the letter, very much indeed; but Jane Austen is too perceptive a reader of character to suppose that all comes clear at once: it is by a marvellous irony that Elizabeth is made to reflect, ' "Had I been in love, I could not have been more wretchedly blind" '; nor, though Elizabeth does know herself henceforth much better, does she yet know herself completely.

It is even true that her attitude toward the letter is to undergo a further change – when she has had a better chance to think of it with some coolness. She almost completely reverses her first excited opinion:

> His attachment excited gratitude, his general character respect; but she could not approve him; nor could she for a moment repent her refusal, or feel the slightest inclination ever to see him

1. *Pride and Prejudice*, p. 208. 2. ibid., p. 208.

again. In her own past behaviour, there was a constant source of vexation and regret; and in the unhappy defects of her family a subject of yet heavier chagrin.[1]

So, in a half-way stage in her thinking and feeling, she yet refuses to look squarely at the consequences of a commitment to Darcy; she still rebels against involvement. Nevertheless, her uncompromising honesty causes her to realize that there is much justice in his views about her family – all of them but Jane.

Elizabeth does not see Darcy again until the unexpected encounter at Pemberley, to which she has gone with the Gardiners on vacation. Presumably she has had an opportunity to absorb the lesson of the letter; at least she is now more willing to believe good things about him – from Mrs Reynolds, for instance, who is the housekeeper of Pemberley and has only warm praise for her master, whom she has known since he was four years old – ' "and he was always the sweetest-tempered, most generous-hearted, boy in the world." '[2]

Already softened towards Darcy by such unstinted praise, she meets him by chance (he has returned home a day early) and finds him more civil to her than ever before, unfailingly kind to the Gardiners, and urgently desirous to ' "introduce my sister to your acquaintance" '.[3] She likes Georgiana, and after the meeting takes occasion to reflect on her own not very clear feelings:

She certainly did not hate him. No; hatred had vanished long ago, and she had almost as long been ashamed of ever feeling a dislike against him, that could be so called. The respect created by the conviction of his valuable qualities, though at first unwillingly admitted, had for some time ceased to be repugnant to her feelings; and it was now heightened into somewhat of a friendlier nature, by the testimony so highly in his favour, and bringing forward his disposition in so amiable a light, which yesterday had produced. But above all, above respect and esteem, there was a motive within her of good will which could not be overlooked. It was gratitude. – Gratitude, not merely for having once loved her,

1. ibid., p. 212. 2. ibid., p. 249. 3. ibid., p. 256.

but for loving her still well enough, to forgive all the petulance and acrimony of her manner in rejecting him, and all the unjust accusations accompanying her rejection. ... She respected, she esteemed, she was grateful to him, she felt a real interest in his welfare; and she only wanted to know how far she wished that welfare to depend upon herself, and how far it would be for the happiness of both that she should employ the power, which her fancy told her she still possessed, of bringing on the renewal of his addresses.[1]

It is in the anti-climax of the first paragraph quoted (respect, esteem – gratitude) that Jane Austen is able to indicate something of the complexity of Elizabeth's mind, and the entire passage shows the continued resistance which she is still putting up against the release of her own strong feelings.

A crisis is called for, something which will break the placidity of her reflections; and this comes in the stunning news that Lydia Bennet and George Wickham have eloped; in her anguish Elizabeth blurts the story out to Darcy, who is most consolatory and kind. Nevertheless, when she leaves Derbyshire – as now she must, hurriedly – she is certain she will never see him again. She feels genuine regret on departure: and her feelings have ascended to another level.

Now the focus of attention shifts from Darcy and Elizabeth to Lydia and the conscienceless militia officer – the search for them in London, the self-recriminations of Mr Bennet, the marriage agreed upon. Elizabeth has little leisure to reflect on her own feelings for several weeks. Then she begins to regret telling Darcy about the elopement, for now that Lydia and Wickham are to be married, she feels that the first tawdry adventure might have been concealed from him, who would so strenuously disapprove – though no doubt he would not under any circumstances ally himself to a family connected in any way with the despicable Wickham.

She began now to comprehend that he [Darcy] was exactly the man, who, in disposition and talents, would most suit her. His

1. *Pride and Prejudice*, pp. 265, 266.

understanding and temper, though unlike her own, would have answered all her wishes. It was an union that must have been to the advantage of both; by her ease and liveliness, his mind might have been softened, his manners improved, and from his judgement, information, and knowledge of the world, she must have received benefit of greater importance.[1]

But now, she thinks, it is too late: such an alliance can never be – until she discovers that it has been Darcy who has been mainly instrumental in arranging the marriage between Lydia and Wickham, through motives which she must interpret in but one way: 'Her heart did whisper, that he had done it for her.' [2] But she still cannot quite believe that he would ever consent to be the brother-in-law of Wickham, even for her. Nevertheless, she refuses – with keen disdain – to promise Lady Catherine de Bourgh not to accept a proposal of marriage from Darcy: an interview which, as Darcy says, ' "taught me to hope . . . as I had scarcely ever allowed myself to hope before" '.[3] And so they are betrothed, at last.

But why has it been so much easier for her to like George Wickham? It is certainly true that, on their first meeting, he is much more polite than Darcy; his façade is much smoother, and his wit just as sharp. Elizabeth herself says, ' "I have courted prepossession and ignorance. . . ." ' But there is a further reason, that she feels no danger of a permanent attachment to him; and for this second reason, she yields all too willingly to the belief that Darcy is what Wickham says he is.

She deceives herself: Mrs Gardiner, who is much more perceptive in this matter than her niece, warns Elizabeth not to fall in love with the lieutenant. But Elizabeth promises only to go slowly. Nevertheless (and this, it seems to me, proves my second point) she feels not a single pang of regret when Wickham announces his engagement to Miss King, the girl with a dowry of £10,000. As she writes to her aunt.

'I am now convinced . . . that I have never been much in love; for had I really experienced that pure and elevating passion, I should

1. ibid., p. 312. 2. ibid., p. 326. 3. ibid., p. 367.

at present detest his very name, and wish him all manner of evil. But my feelings are not only cordial towards *him*; they are even impartial towards Miss King. . . . There can be no love in all this.' [1]

And she is right: so she can afford herself the luxury of deciding, before leaving for Kent, that Wickham 'must always be her model of the amiable and pleasing'; [2] she can (or so she thinks) indulge herself in the imperception of denying to Mrs Gardiner that Wickham's attachment discloses his mercenary motives.

The profundity of her mortification at knowing the truth about him comes, then, not merely from the knowledge that her perceptions, on which she has prided herself, have been beclouded by prejudice, but from the deeper reason that her relationship to him, because it has not engaged her much, has been able to afford the luxury of quasi-intimacy. Against clarity, in *Pride and Prejudice,* involvement is set: both are desirable, but each, ironically, works against the other – and the reader cannot believe that the marriage of Darcy and Elizabeth, however happy or beneficial, will ever quite close the breach between these two opposites.

Fitzwilliam Darcy and George Wickham

In *Pride and Prejudice,* hero and villain have prominent, interesting, and convincing parts. Each is present throughout the novel, both attract the heroine, and both receive the marital fates which they deserve. Elizabeth Bennet is a complicated and penetrating heroine; the two men with whom she associates herself romantically must also be intricate and intelligent.

If (as we have shown) Elizabeth's prejudices are views in which she takes pride, so ought it be said that Darcy's pride leads to prejudice. But even this is an over-simplification: his austerity of manner, as we learn from his housekeeper at Pemberley, stems partly from an inordinate shyness. It is impossible, however, to explain away his famous remark about Elizabeth '"... tolerable; but not handsome enough to tempt

1. *Pride and Prejudice,* p. 150. 2. ibid., p. 152.

me ..." '[1] on the grounds of diffidence alone – nor, indeed, the statement that '"My good opinion once lost is lost for ever,' "[2] nor the first proposal to Elizabeth; nor his subsequent explanatory letter. He *is* a proud man.

One way in which Jane Austen delineates his character is through his relationship with Bingley.[3] It is partly through this friendship that a certain completeness is given to Darcy's character. Although we are struck, at the very beginning of the book, with Darcy's rudeness and with his pride, we may overlook the solidity of temperament implied in his affection for Bingley.

Despite his early bad impression of Elizabeth, he is soon constrained to like her better: for, ironically, the heroine by behaving disdainfully to him, does just what is necessary to captivate him. Thus at Sir William Lucas's party, her refusal to dance with him only sets him to thinking of her attractiveness; her piquancy at Netherfield leads to the famous conversation in which Elizabeth, while acknowledging that '"I dearly love a laugh"', insists that '"I hope I never ridicule what is wise or good"'[4] – and from there to Darcy's increased awareness of 'the danger of paying Elizabeth too much attention'.[5]

The next appearance of Darcy comes when Elizabeth is visiting Hunsford, where she has gone to fulfil an unwilling promise of spending some time with Charlotte and William Collins. Besides the unfortunate first impression which the squire of Pemberley has made, there is now the insistent and plausible evidence against his character which Wickham has adduced. Elizabeth cannot understand the why of Darcy's repeated calls at the parsonage, nor can she comprehend the astonishing regularity of their 'unexpected' encounters in the Park. And she is stunned by his declaration of love, and

1. *Pride and Prejudice*, p. 12. This remark, however, does little more than show him to be out of humour. The reader should not make Elizabeth's mistake of judging him too hardly for it.

2. ibid., p. 58. 3. See above, p. 32. 4. *Pride and Prejudice*, p. 57.
5. ibid., p. 58.

proposal of marriage (critics who censure Jane Austen for an alleged lack of emotion should re-read this chapter).

Elizabeth's astonishment was beyond expression. She stared, coloured, doubted, and was silent. This he considered sufficient encouragement, and the avowal of all that he felt, and had long felt for her, immediately followed. He spoke well, but there were feelings besides those of the heart to be detailed, and he was not more eloquent on the subject of tenderness than of pride. His sense of her inferiority – of its being a degradation – of the family obstacles which judgement had always opposed to inclination, were dwelt on with a warmth which seemed due to the consequence he was wounding, but was very unlikely to recommend his suit.

In spite of her deeply-rooted dislike, she could not be insensible to the compliment of such a man's affection, and though her intentions did not vary for an instant, she was at first sorry for the pain he was to receive; till, roused to resentment by his subsequent language, she lost all compassion in anger. She tried, however, to compose herself to answer him with patience, when he should have done. He concluded with representing to her the strength of that attachment which, in spite of all his endeavours, he had found impossible to conquer; and with expressing his hope that it would now be rewarded by her acceptance of his hand. As he said this, she could easily see that he had no doubt of a favourable answer. He *spoke* of apprehension and anxiety, but his countenance expressed real security. Such a circumstance could only exasperate farther . . .[1]

Elizabeth's angry refusal marks the beginning of the great change in Darcy: he is humbled, though there is but one sentence in the letter which he writes to her, to indicate that he has been mollified: 'I will only add, God bless you.' [2]

Now he disappears from view, until Elizabeth, together with the Gardiners, visits Pemberley. Here Elizabeth's opinion of him softens slightly. And in fact there is a series of circumstances which disclose him to be a much more human person than she has previously thought him.

But this is not all: he behaves heroically, for he hastens to

1. *Pride and Prejudice*, p. 189. 2. ibid., p. 203.

London, seeks out Lydia and Wickham, makes a provision for them, and all but drags them to the altar. These things he does not out of admiration for the eloped couple, but out of love for Elizabeth – which, however, he does not again bring himself to declare, until after Lady Catherine de Bourgh's interview with Elizabeth. This '"taught me to hope"',[1] and so he is able to propose again, this time with success.

George Wickham is at once the most plausible and the most villainous of Jane Austen's anti-heroes: he is handsome, persuasive, personable; disingenuous, calculating, and dishonourable. His appearance in the story comes just as Elizabeth, smarting from Darcy's disapprobation, willingly abrogates her critical faculties in favour of a pleasant countenance and manner. She all too readily believes the militia lieutenant's defamation of Darcy's character – though we, the readers, are expected to take note of the warning signals which Elizabeth ignores. In the first place, Jane Bennet declares:

> 'It is impossible. No man of common humanity, no man who had any value for his character, could be capable of it. Can his most intimate friends be so excessively deceived in him? Oh! no.'[2]

In the second place, Miss Bingley plainly warns Elizabeth about Wickham, and indicates his relationship to Darcy:

> 'So, Miss Eliza, I hear you are quite delighted with George Wickham! – Your sister has been talking to me about him, and asking me a thousand questions; and I find that the young man forgot to tell you, among his other communications, that he was the son of old Wickham, the late Mr Darcy's steward. Let me recommend you, however, as a friend, not to give implicit confidence to all his assertions; for as to Mr Darcy's using him ill, it is perfectly false; for, on the contrary, he has been always remarkably kind to him, though George Wickham has treated Mr Darcy in a most infamous manner.'[3]

Jane Austen does not stack the cards, but she is not averse to throwing sand in her readers' eyes: both Jane and Miss Bingley are, as it happens, perfectly correct here; but Elizabeth does

1. ibid., p. 367. 2. ibid., p. 85. 3. ibid., p. 94.

not believe either of them, for Jane's unwillingness ever to be unkind does sometimes blind her to people's faults, and Caroline Bingley's careless, insensitive stupidity often leads to complete misapprehension.

So Elizabeth continues to think well of Wickham, and ill of Darcy – even when the former announces his engagement to Miss King, whose dowry is £10,000. This time the heroine ignores the testimony – or rather, the conjecture – of one whose judgement she has always trusted: her aunt, Mrs Gardiner.

'If [says Mrs Gardiner] you will only tell me what sort of girl Miss King is, I shall know what to think.'

'She is a very good kind of girl, I believe. I know no harm of her.'

'But he paid her not the smallest attention, till her grandfather's death made her mistress of this fortune.'

'No – why should he? If it was not allowable for him to gain *my* affections, because I had no money, what occasion could there be for making love to a girl whom he did not care about, and who was equally poor?'

'But there seems indelicacy in directing his attentions towards her, so soon after this event.'

'A man in distressed circumstances has not time for all those elegant decorums which other people may observe. If *she* does not object to it, why should *we*?'

'*Her* not objecting, does not justify *him*. It only shews her being deficient in something herself – sense or feeling.'

'Well,' cried Elizabeth, 'have it as you choose. *He* shall be mercenary, and *she* shall be foolish.' [1]

Although she is still unbelieving, however, Elizabeth will remember the doubts which she quashed in her early enthusiasm for Wickham – which, after all, arose partly out of her disdain for Darcy. Her big change dates from her second reading of Darcy's letter; then she excoriates herself for her blindness – though she cannot be expected to have guessed the full measure of Wickham's evil: his complete misrepresenta-

1. *Pride and Prejudice*, p. 153.

tion of Darcy, his planned elopement with Georgiana, his dissipated existence in London.

He gets the fate which he deserves: he marries Lydia, after causing great distress to everyone concerned, except the foolish young girl herself. But, true to his character, he does not lose an ounce of aplomb. On this visit to Longbourn:

his manners were always so pleasing, that had his character and his marriage been exactly what they ought, his smiles and his easy address, while he claimed their relationship, would have delighted them all. Elizabeth had not before believed him quite equal to such assurance; but she sat down, resolving within herself, to draw no limits in future to the impudence of an impudent man.[1]

Darcy and Wickham are virtually perfect agents of illusionment, and thus of the ironic theme, in *Pride and Prejudice*. Elizabeth is put off by Darcy's rudeness; her vanity is piqued: but she allows herself to over-emphasize his pride, because she comes so dangerously near to involvement with him. She credits Wickham's testimony because it is congenial to her – she misapprehends him because she wants to avoid entanglement with Darcy, while in fact there is nothing to fear from her relationship to Wickham: she is essentially indifferent to him. Thus her clarity of perception, which she genuinely possesses, contains the germs of its own myopia – ironically, when engagement of her affections is threatened.

4. MANSFIELD PARK

Fanny Price

Mansfield Park provides enduring proof that Jane Austen is not always ironic, for, although the novel is not without fine touches of irony (particularly in the characterizations of Aunt Norris, of Sir Thomas Bertram, and of the Crawfords), the two central characters are presented straightforwardly, entirely without contradiction of any kind. Edmund Bertram is doubtless one of the dullest figures in the entire Austenian canon;

1. ibid., p. 316.

Fanny is saved that fate by a sympathetic presentation, though at times she is too insufferably good to be acceptable even to the enthusiast. The heroines of all the other novels (if my theory of the double protagonist in *Sense and Sensibility* be admissible) have a certain rebelliousness – from the violent woman-of-feeling Marianne Dashwood and the Gothic-infected Catherine Morland, through the prejudiced Elizabeth Bennet and the God-playing Emma Woodhouse, to the finally independent Anne Elliot. Only Fanny is a simple accepting figure, and the message is: good girls come out best, after all.

Females of Fanny's type usually have a hard row to hoe in fiction, harder, it may be, than in real life: but perhaps one seldom meets a Sophia Western, an Evelina, a Jeanie Deans, a Lucy Desborough, or an Amelia Sedley. In varying degrees they are all – including Fanny Price – naïve, sweet, honest, and courageous; and unless they are presented with a good deal of imagination, they are apt to be uninteresting. Miss Austen's heroine comes off pretty well, partly because her author places her among people who are bound to compel our interest, partly because she is not sentimentalized (for instance, she is appalled by her visit to Portsmouth), and partly because she has, like Anne Elliot, a compelling sweetness which takes us over such bumps as her objections to producing a play at Mansfield Park.

When she first arrives at Mansfield – she is a slight girl of ten years, 'exceedingly timid and shy, and shrinking from notice' – she comes under a shadow: that of charity, for she is taken by the Bertrams (and ostensibly by Mrs Norris) out of pity for her mother who has produced eight children in eleven years and has another on the way. But before she even has time to be frightened by Lady Bertram's silence, awed by Sir Thomas's grave looks, and teased by the Bertram children, she is made miserable by her Aunt Norris, who:

> ... had been talking to her the whole way from Northampton of her wonderful good fortune, and the extraordinary degree of gratitude and good behaviour which it ought to produce, and her

consciousness of misery was therefore increased by the idea of its being a wicked thing for her not to be happy.[1]

Only Edmund provides some consolation for her distress – first by inquiring after her family, then by fetching her some stationery with which to write to her beloved brother William, and always subsequently by treating her with a consideration and an affection of which all the other members of the family seem quite incapable. Not only does Mrs Norris continually remind her of her 'place', but Maria and Julia Bertram wilfully ignore her, 'and it is not very wonderful that with all their promising talents and early information, they should be entirely deficient in the less common acquirements of self-knowledge, generosity, and humility.' [2]

Thus is Fanny introduced, rather conventionally it must be admitted: and throughout the book there is never any question of self-contradiction in her character; she behaves with a consistency, a steadiness, which quite plainly show an unquestioned set of values. On the other hand, she is no mere wooden humour; she is not simply an inanimate vehicle for Jane Austen's moralizing. This point can be illustrated in several ways – but I shall choose her relationship to the production of *Lovers' Vows*, her attitude to Henry Crawford, and her reaction to her family at Portsmouth, when she goes to visit them as a young woman, after having been at Mansfield Park for several years.

Fanny stands alone in her unqualified disapproval of putting on a play at Mansfield Park. The idea comes from the Honourable John Yates, a young man visiting Tom Bertram. As might be expected, the Miss Bertrams quickly fall into line; 'and Henry Crawford, to whom, in all the riot of his gratifications, it was yet an untasted pleasure, was quite alive at the idea.' [3] Mary Crawford follows suit, and even Mrs Norris lends her weight (principally the sheer weight of talkiness) to the scheme. Edmund, though he disapproves, is gradually

1. *Mansfield Park*, p. 13. The other quotations in this paragraph come, respectively, from pp. 12 and 14.

2. ibid., p. 19. 3. ibid., p. 123.

persuaded by the others. Only Fanny holds out against the plan – and this has often been remarked as a paradox in Jane Austen, who liked theatricals, and whose family is known to have put on amateur performances at home.[1] But, as Dr Chapman points out, there are at least two very good reasons why Fanny should demur: first, the accurate (as it turns out) suspicion that Sir Thomas, who is absent, would disapprove; and second, the very awkward situations arising from such (apparent) necessities as casting Henry Crawford opposite Maria Bertram, who is engaged to James Rushworth.[2]

Fanny maintains her resistance throughout the early stages, will not play the part of the Cottager's wife, shrinks with horror for more reasons than one when Mary Crawford seeks her out and will practise the love scene she is to play opposite Edmund. Yet at the crucial moment – on the day of the final rehearsal, when Mrs Grant fails to appear to play the part of the Cottager's wife – Fanny is persuaded to read the lines, though with great reluctance.

> ... as Edmund repeated his wish, and with a look of even fond dependence on her good nature, she must yield. She would do her best. Every body was satisfied – and she was left to the tremors of a most palpitating heart, while the others prepared to begin.[3]

The fact that she yields here cannot argue, if this section of the book is read carefully, a weak moral structure so far as Fanny is concerned: she never weakens for a moment in her disapprobation; but her acquiescence at last gives a human

1. R. W. Chapman, *Jane Austen Facts and Problems*, pp. 197, 198.

2. ibid., p. 198. Dr Chapman makes an additional point which is of interest. 'The class to which Jane Austen and her Bertrams belonged regarded the aristocracy with suspicious hostility. Now *Lovers' Vows* was under that cloud; it was introduced by an Hon. John Yates ... from a country-house performance the cast of which had included a duke. But dukes as a class, and baronets and country parsons as a class, were then remote from each other; the former class despised its inferiors, and the inferiors retorted with moral reprobation' (pp. 198, 199). *Lovers' Vows* itself, containing seduction and bastardy, is also repugnant because of its subject-matter.

3. *Mansfield Park*, p. 172.

dimension to her character, not always achieved in the portrayal of her type in fiction.

Her relationship to Henry Crawford is another case in point. She disapproves of him from the very beginning, and for reasons that can hardly seem bad even in the morally indifferent twentieth century: she sees him flirt overtly with Maria Bertram, whose engagement to James Rushworth is a matter of common knowledge. She thinks him a trifler, he whose '" plan is to make Fanny Price fall in love with me" '.[1] She stands out against him, despite the most ardent pressure from him (he actually does fall in love with her), and the most heated persuasions of both Sir Thomas and Edmund. She must feel gratitude toward him, for he obtains a lieutenant's commission for her sailor brother; she must resist his declaration of love and proposal of marriage – not once but twice; and she must endure the terrifying disapproval of Sir Thomas:

> 'I had thought you peculiarly free from wilfulness of temper, self-conceit. ... But you have now shewn me that you can be wilful and perverse, that you can and will decide for yourself, without any consideration or deference for those who have surely some right to guide you – without even asking their advice. ... You think only of yourself; and because you do not feel for Mr Crawford exactly what a young, heated fancy imagines to be necessary for happiness, you resolve to refuse him at once. ... You do not owe me the duty of a child. But Fanny, if your heart can acquit you of *gratitude* –'[2]

She does all these things with a steadfastness that can no doubt be mocked at, but with a courage that can hardly be despised.

But the development – and the denouement – of this situation discloses in Fanny a human dimension: for after she has been for a month in Portsmouth where the noisome atmosphere appals her, and after she is finally forced to abandon her hope that Edmund will not marry Miss Crawford, she begins to change somewhat her opinion of Henry.

1. ibid., p. 229. 2. ibid., pp. 318, 319.

The wonderful improvement which she still fancied in Mr Crawford, was the nearest to administering comfort of anything within the current of her thoughts. Not considering in how different a circle she had been just seeing him, nor how much might be owed to contrast, she was quite persuaded of his being astonishingly more gentle, and regardful of others, than formerly. And if in little things, must it not be so in great? [1]

Here, it seems to me, is a delicate balance of faithfulness (in her love for Edmund) and a very human change of mind.

Portsmouth is largely responsible for the latter. This episode, which dominates the third volume of the novel, is solid testimony of Jane Austen's realism. Fanny returns there to visit her family, from whom she has been separated for nearly a decade. A sentimental novelist would have thrown a veil over the poverty, the dirt, and the rudeness. But Fanny finds a cramped house, the atmosphere of which is confused and inefficient; a bedraggled mother; a coarse-talking and foul-smelling father; and 'two rosy-faced boys, ragged and dirty'. After a week, Fanny reflects that her home is

in almost every respect, the very reverse of what she could have wished. It was the abode of noise, disorder, and impropriety. Nobody was in their right place, nothing was done as it ought to be. She could not respect her parents, as she had hoped. . . . [Her father was] dirty and gross . . . [and her mother was] always busy without getting on, always behindhand and lamenting it, without altering her ways; wishing to be an economist, without contrivance or regularity; dissatisfied with her servants, without skill to make them better, and whether helping, or reprimanding, or indulging them, without any power of engaging their respect.[2]

And by the end of two months, when at last she is summoned back to Mansfield Park, she is delighted to go. So she quite exceeds, in the reader's mind, the boundaries of a mere type. She has 'gentleness, virtue, wisdom, and endurance', but she has very honestly unelevated responses as well.

In the nineteenth century *Mansfield Park* vied with *Pride and Prejudice* for the first place in the hearts of Jane Austen's

1. *Mansfield Park*, pp. 413, 414. 2. ibid., pp. 381, 388–90.

readers![1] Nowadays, many people would tend to agree with Lord David Cecil that Fanny Price is 'a little wooden, a little charmless, and rather a prig'.[2] By comparison to the other heroines she certainly is. But Fanny, though she is not ironically treated, deserves a sympathetic consideration which will enable the reader to see her as a truly three-dimensional figure.[3]

Edmund Bertram and Henry Crawford

Of all Jane Austen's heroes, Edmund Bertram is the one least likely to capture our sympathy or affection; of all her villains, Henry Crawford is the one most apt to elicit such comment as the following, by Lord David Cecil:

> ... Henry Crawford comes to life as a sympathetic character; and under the pressure of his personality the plot takes a turn, of which the only logical conclusion is his marriage with the heroine Fanny. ... In the last three chapters [however] she [Jane Austen] violently wrenches the story back into its original course: but only at the cost of making Henry act in a manner wholly inconsistent with the rest of his character.[4]

But, although Edmund is a prig, his author does not paint him a paragon, as (especially) his infatuation with Mary Crawford shows; nor does the book itself yield any conclusive evidence that Henry Crawford was ever meant to be anything but a villain: on the contrary, it is plain throughout that his final piece of folly is wholly consonant with the character that Jane Austen has drawn of him.

Edmund, it is true, does first appear as all that is good. By his unfailing kindness and tact, he soon wins a place in Fanny's heart second only to her greatly beloved brother William. But even before his attachment to Mary Crawford, he shows

1. A. C. Bradley points this fact out, but himself prefers *Pride and Prejudice*. See his 'Jane Austen', in *Essays and Studies by Members of the English Association*, II (1911), pp. 7–36.

2. *Jane Austen* (Leslie Stephen Lecture, 1935), Cambridge, 1936, p. 12.

3. The rehabilitation of Fanny has been greatly facilitated by Lionel Trilling's brilliant essay on *Mansfield Park* in *The Opposing Self*, London, 1955, pp. 206–30.

4. *Jane Austen*, 1936, p. 19.

us something of a straightforward honesty which will not be obscured by the demands of convention. *After* his sister Maria's engagement to James Rushworth has been made generally known, he remarks: '"If this man had not twelve thousand a year, he would be a very stupid fellow."' [1] And at that moment the reader is able to extend to him a hitherto withheld sympathy. Edmund's quietly effected arrangements for Fanny to go to Sotherton also exact our approbation.

But it is in relation to Mary Crawford that he emerges most fully as a human being with quite usual (and quite un-paragonic) blindnesses and self-deceptions. From the moment of her arrival he is bewitched – so much so that he forgets Fanny's claims to one of his mares, and allows Miss Crawford to ride it whenever she pleases. In fact, for four days, he quite neglects poor Fanny until, owing to Aunt Norris's stupidity and Lady Bertram's lassitudinous observations on Fanny's want of complexion, he is made to realize that he has been negligent.

He is, however, to go further: he is to allow his own good judgement to be quite overthrown by Mary Crawford. While his father is in Antigua, Edmund has a large share of the responsibility for seeing that things run properly at Mansfield Park. When the plan of putting on a play is suggested, he disapproves strongly – and feels that his father would also disapprove. But when Mary Crawford lends her approbation, 'the scheme was advanced'.[2] He even allows himself to be overridden as to the choice of a play, though he finds *Lovers' Vows* shocking. And to cap all, he plays a love-scene with Mary.

Chapter after chapter, his courtship of her continues, even in the face of her disapproval of the clergy, and her entreaties that he will not be ordained, but will instead go into another – any other – profession. The desire to stand well with her even causes him to try to persuade Fanny to accept Henry Crawford:

'He is lively, you are serious; but so much the better; his spirits will support yours. It is your disposition to be easily dejected, and to fancy difficulties greater than they are. His cheerfulness will

1. *Mansfield Park*, p. 40. 2. ibid., p. 129.

counteract this. He sees difficulties nowhere; and his pleasantness and gaiety will be a constant support to you.' [1]

But, as Fanny points out to him:

> 'I *should* have thought . . . that every woman must have felt the possibility of a man's not being approved, not being loved by someone of her sex, at least, let him be ever so generally agreeable. Let him have all the perfections in the world, I think it ought not to be set down as certain, that a man must be acceptable to every woman he may happen to like himself.' [2]

Edmund, then, hardly behaves with the unclouded (if narrow) vision of the ideal clergyman. For Mary Crawford's sake, he is willing not to make allowances but to be dishonest with himself. He '"cannot give her up"' [3] until she tries to condone the scandalous elopement of her brother with Maria Rushworth, by calling it 'folly'.

> '... no reluctance, no horror ... no modest loathings! – This is what the world does. For where, Fanny, shall we find a woman whom nature had so richly endowed? – Spoilt, spoilt! –' [4]

It must be admitted, however, that Henry Crawford is a good deal more interesting than his opposite number. He has something of Henry Tilney's turn for irony, and a certain glitter which Edmund certainly lacks. In conception and in execution, however, Henry Crawford is meant to be a villain – though, as Miss Austen quite appropriately shows us, even a villain may have some good qualities.[5]

Almost at once he shows his hand. On the pilgrimage to Sotherton, he impudently flirts with Maria Bertram, who is known to be engaged to James Rushworth – and when the latter's back is turned, they disappear into the 'wilderness', thus angering Fanny and mortifying Mr Rushworth. He is

1. ibid., p. 348. 2. ibid., p. 353.
3. ibid., p. 422. 4. ibid., p. 455.
5. Compare Sheila Kaye-Smith and G. B. Stern, with whose view I disagree. Henry Crawford, they say, 'was not rubbish; fundamentally he had plenty of character and strength of purpose.' *Talking of Jane Austen*, London, 1943, p. 49. They feel that Fanny should have married him.

equally ready to throw propriety aside when the question of the theatricals comes up: and he even insists on playing opposite Maria in *Lovers' Vows.* He is hard-hearted enough to remark later on the unseasonableness of Sir Thomas's arrival, '"I think, Miss Price, we would have indulged ourselves with a week's calm in the Atlantic at that season."' [1] Thus Jane Austen delicately exposes Henry's deficiency of moral taste, and so, here as elsewhere, prefigures Henry James.

There is little cause, therefore, to suppose Henry Crawford anything like a heroic character. On the other hand, his love for Fanny – which develops only after he has decided to trifle with her affections – is genuinely moving, and at the same time consonant with one side of his personality. Here he appears at his most attractive: helping William Price to get a commission in the Navy, attentive and devoted to Fanny, overwhelmed with surprise when she refuses him, finally jarred into some self-awareness after her repeated denials of him.

> 'Well,' said Crawford, after a course of rapid questions and reluctant answers – 'I am happier than I was, because I now understand more clearly your opinion of me. You think me unsteady – easily swayed by the whim of the moment – easily tempted – easily put aside. With such an opinion, no wonder that – But we shall see. – It is not by protestations that I shall endeavour to convince you I am wronged, it is not by telling you that my affections are steady. My conduct shall speak for me – absence, distance, time, shall speak for me. – *They* shall prove ... I do deserve you.' [2]

And for a while, spurred by his love for Fanny, Henry does try to change. At Portsmouth, he is unfailingly sweet and kind to her – but when he returns to London he also reverts to his old self. His elopement with Maria is an unsurprising finale to an unpromising beginning – though his author tells us that, had he married Fanny, 'there would have been every probability of success and felicity for him. His affection had already done something.' [3] But this was not to be.

Mansfield Park, then, cannot be called an ironic novel. Like

1. *Mansfield Park*, p. 225. 2. ibid., p. 343. 3. ibid., p. 467.

the fragmentary *Lady Susan* it lacks that dimension. Want of breeding is responsible for the evils in Henry Crawford, as in all the other bad characters; good breeding supports and develops Fanny and Edmund. So this work can only be contrasted to the rest of the canon: it is much darker than Jane Austen's other novels; it is none the less delicate, honest, subtle.

5. EMMA

Emma Woodhouse

Emma Woodhouse is young, rich, intelligent, beautiful, charming, perceptive, and gay; but she is vain of her own perceptions, snobbish, domineering, rash, and selfish. She is kind to her father, charitable to the poor, fond of Mr Knightley, and attached to 'poor Miss Taylor'. But her misapprehensions – of Harriet, of Mr Elton, of Jane Fairfax, of Frank Churchill, of Mr Knightley, and of herself – lead her to develop and encourage a number of situations which, however amusing, clearly display the profound contradictions which are the essence of irony. 'I am going', said Jane Austen in a letter, 'to take a heroine whom no one but myself will much like,' and we must agree with Howells that 'it took supreme courage to portray a girl, meant to win and keep the reader's fancy, with the characteristics frankly ascribed to Emma Woodhouse. ... An officious and self-confident girl, even if pretty, is not usually one to take the fancy, and yet Emma takes the fancy.' [1]

Emma is, like all great heroes, the victim of her own illusions: she creates a world, but it is not the real world. How deceptive is appearance, and how misleading. One could make the same exclamation about Othello or Lear. Still, it would be a mere over-simplification to say that the book turns on the contrast of appearance to reality: too simple because, though the statement is true, the significance of the novel –

1. Jane Austen quoted in James Edward Austen-Leigh, *A Memoir of Jane Austen*, 2nd ed., London, 1871, p. 148; Howells, op. cit., I, pp. 66, 67.

as in Shakespeare – lies in the variety of illusions and in the complexity of reality.

The first volume of the novel concerns itself with the Harriet Smith–Mr Elton débâcle; and here we come to know the Emma of supreme self-confidence and serene delusion. 'The real evils indeed of Emma's situation were the power of having rather too much her own way, and a disposition to think a little too well of herself.' [1] These are now, however, 'unperceived'. She asserts to Mr Knightley that the one consoling feature of poor Miss Taylor's marriage to Mr Weston is ' "that I made the match myself" ',[2] and although the squire of Donwell replies that Emma's part in the match is much less than she imagines, she – quite characteristically – pays little attention and then goes on to say that she will make one more match, that of Mr Elton, vicar of Highbury. Again she is warned, again in vain: ' "Invite him to dinner, Emma, and help him to the best of the fish and the chicken, but leave him to chuse his own wife. Depend upon it, a man of six or seven-and-twenty can take care of himself." ' [3]

And so by the end of the first chapter the stage is set for Emma's first great mistake – all is set, except that the heroine has not yet found the lady to whom Mr Elton must become attached. She soon appears in the person of Harriet Smith, 'the natural daughter of somebody'.[4] Surely no more likely a choice could be possible than this placid, sweet-tempered girl whom Emma resolves to 'notice'. She quickly takes her in hand, and turns her life upside down. In the first place she must quash the relationship of Harriet to the Martins of Abbey-Mill Farm, whom Harriet has recently visited with great pleasure:

'The yeomanry are precisely the order of people with whom I feel I can have nothing to do. A degree or two lower, and a creditable appearance might interest me; I might hope to be useful to their families in some way or other. But a farmer can need none

1. *Emma*, p. 5. 2. ibid., p. 11.
3. ibid., p. 14. 4. ibid., p. 22.

of my help, and is therefore in one sense as much above my notice as in every other he is below it.' [1]

And although her protégée has been favourably impressed with Robert Martin, Emma dashes cold water on any possible connexion to him: '"I want to see you permanently well connected – and to that end it will be advisable to have as few odd acquaintance as may be...."' [2] But mere conversation is not enough, and so when Emma sees Robert Martin, she disapproves him to Harriet rather more than sincerity would otherwise permit.

Thus within four chapters Emma has determined that she will get Mr Elton attached, has chosen the girl, and has detached the latter from the only person capable (she thinks) of spoiling the plan. The next task is to arouse Mr Elton's interest; but first we are permitted to overhear a conversation between Mrs Weston and Mr Knightley, the latter insisting that the relationship of Emma and Harriet is bad for both girls:

'How can Emma imagine she has any thing to learn herself, while Harriet is presenting such a delightful inferiority? And as for Harriet, I will venture to say that she cannot gain by the acquaintance. Hartfield will only put her out of conceit with all the other places she belongs to.' [3]

This is a perfectly accurate statement of the facts of the situation, and a faultless forecast of the future. But Mr Knightley is the Cassandra of this piece: Mrs Weston, blinded by affection, pooh-poohs him, while Emma, intoxicated by a false view of her own power, proceeds logically to put her plan in action.

She turns to Mr Elton and virtually demands that he praise Harriet:

'You have given Miss Smith all that she required,' said he; 'you have made her graceful and easy. She was a beautiful creature when she came to you, but, in my opinion, the attractions you

1. ibid., p. 29. 2. ibid., p. 31. 3. ibid., p. 38.

have added are infinitely superior to what she received from nature.'[1]

This passage is retrospectively ironic – as indeed is the whole fabric of Emma's relationship to the vicar in this period. How, let us pause to ask, can she be so mistaken? First, of course, because her desire to effect the attachment makes her ignore all negative evidence. But there is another cause as well: Emma's removal of herself from any possibility of involvement. Mr Elton 'was reckoned very handsome; his person much admired in general, though not by her, there being a want of elegance of feature which she could not dispense with: – but the girl who could be gratified by a Robert Martin's riding about the country to get walnuts for her, might very well be conquered by Mr Elton's admiration.'[2] This refusal of involvement is by no means less important than her vanity in her misconstruction of experience. Thus, later, her disapprobation of Jane Fairfax and Mr Knightley as a possible combination (and afterwards of Harriet and the same gentleman) is grounded (spuriously) on the wish that 'poor little Henry', John Knightley's son, must have Donwell; her inexperience at personal implication causes her to believe, though only briefly, that she is in love with Frank Churchill: she is simply unacquainted with the symptoms. And what happens in the novel, so far as Emma is concerned, might be said to be the exorcism of her pride of power together with the growing realization that she must become tangled in the skein of relationships in which she finds herself: she must not simply direct, she must participate.

To get back to the story: Emma contrives to arouse Mr Elton's interest in Harriet by drawing a picture of the girl. It seems to her an excellent stratagem, for he praises the sketch extravagantly and even offers to take it to London

1. *Emma*, p. 42.

2. ibid., p. 35. Emma, of course, is not attracted by him, nor (as is shown later) does she think of his aspiring to her hand. But now she wishes to dominate, and does not allow herself involvement even with the attractive and suitable Mr Knightley.

to be framed. Both the praise and the offer strike Emma as being evidence of his warming affection for Harriet. She is dead wrong, utterly unaware that the evidence may equally well be evaluated in quite another way – so unaware that she forthwith burns a bridge. The day that Mr Elton is in London, Harriet receives from Robert Martin a letter containing 'a direct proposal of Marriage'. It is, we are told, a splendid letter, though we do not see it (compare *The Ambassadors*, where Mrs Newsome's centrally important letter to Lambert Strether is discussed at length but never transcribed for the reader). Harriet seems anxious that Emma advise her to accept the proposal; but Emma, having already dismissed the Martins, pretends that Harriet is requesting assistance only in the matter of the wording of the reply. The letter to Robert Martin is therefore one of refusal, and 'though Emma continued to protest against any assistance being wanted, it was in fact given in the formation of every sentence.'[1] And Emma, to assuage her friend's disappointment, assures her that the picture which Mr Elton has taken to London will be 'his solace, his delight'.[2] Indeed it will be, but for quite a different reason from what Emma supposes.

It is still, however, early enough for Emma to change her plan, if she wishes. For Harriet, though she has broken with Robert Martin, has yet to be persuaded to love Mr Elton. At this point, Mr Knightley enters, and discloses to Emma that he has encouraged Robert Martin to make the proposal. When he finds not only that it has been refused, but that Emma has so advised Harriet, he is furious. Emma, however, does not desire to have her own eyes opened; and after Mr Knightley asserts that Robert Martin is, in relation to Harriet, ' "as much her superior in sense as in situation" ', Emma is so angry that she replies, ' "Were you, yourself, ever to marry, she is the very woman for you," '[3] – thus revealing how large a part unconsciousness plays in her relationship to Mr Knightley: later, when the marriage of Harriet to him seems a real threat,

1. ibid., p. 55. 2. ibid., p. 56. 3. ibid., pp. 61 and 64 respectively.

Emma learns to know herself better. Meanwhile, he specifically warns her that, if she is going to try match-making for Harriet, she had better not consider Mr Elton:

'Depend upon it, Elton will not do. Elton is a very good sort of man, and a very respectable vicar of Highbury, but not at all likely to make an imprudent match. He knows the value of a good income as well as anybody. Elton may talk sentimentally, but he will act rationally. He is as well acquainted with his own claims, as you can be with Harriet's.' [1]

Yet Emma, despite her respect for Mr Knightley's judgement, refuses to believe in it now. She still could withdraw and persuade Harriet that Mr Elton is not the man for her; instead, she persuades herself that 'Mr Knightley did not make due allowance for the influence of a strong passion at war with all interested motives'.[2] Thus, Mr Knightley's advice, by vexing her deeply, has the reverse of the effect intended: Emma proceeds all the more steadfastly in her scheme.

In the next few days, she becomes increasingly certain that Mr Elton is yielding to her plan. The picture comes back from London elegantly framed: this, she feels, is one sign of his affection for Harriet. Next, in the midst of a vogue of charades the vicar composes one meaning 'courtship'. Emma is sure this is meant for Harriet – while the latter flutters:

'Whatever you say is always right,' cried Harriet, 'and therefore I suppose, and believe, and hope it must be so; but otherwise I could not have imagined it. It is so much beyond any thing I deserve. Mr Elton, who might marry any body! There cannot be two opinions about *him*. He is so very superior. Only think of those sweet verses. ... Dear me, how clever! – Could it really be meant for me?' [3]

The answer to Harriet's question is, of course, that it could not: but Harriet is stupid, and Emma, as usual, the victim of her own delusion. She even copies the charade (all but the last two lines, omitted in the interests of delicacy) into Harriet's book – so that there will be no imputation of forward-

1. *Emma*, p. 66. 2. ibid., p. 67. 3. ibid., p. 74.

ness to the girl; and when Mr Elton, learning of Emma's action, declares this to be '"the proudest moment of his life"', she reflects both on her success in annealing his attachment to Harriet, and on the laughable 'parade' in his manner.

Now, in Emma's own view, everything has been accomplished except the actual proposal, so she will contrive to arrange a *tête-à-tête* meeting of Mr Elton and Harriet. She finds she must negotiate for more than one, however, for nothing seems to happen when she leaves the two of them alone for a few moments on the path by the vicarage. Instead, she 'experienced some disappointment when she found that he was only giving his fair companion an account of the yesterday's party at his friend Cole's, and that she was come in herself for the Stilton cheese, the north Wiltshire, the butter, the cellery, the beet-root and all the desert'.[1] Undaunted, she breaks her shoelace, and contrives to go to Mr Elton's housekeeper for assistance, thus leaving the couple alone for an additional ten minutes – but again nothing happens.

Still, however, though every thing had not been accomplished by her ingenious device, she could not but flatter herself that it had been the occasion of much present enjoyment to both, and must be leading them forward to the great event.[2]

These circumstances, then, though at variance with her plan, do not warn Emma that something may be wrong, or that she should abandon the project. In fact, it is now too late to change the course of events; she has been the prime mover, but they are no longer in her control. So, with a good deal of hard-heartedness, she stifles her contrition at the news that Robert Martin is grievously disappointed by Harriet's refusal. She even ignores John Knightley (who, with his family, has come to visit), when he points out to Emma that Mr Elton '"seems to have a great deal of good-will towards *you*"'.[3]

'I thank you; but I assure you that you are quite mistaken. Mr Elton and I are very good friends, and nothing more;' and she walked on, amusing herself in the consideration of the blunders

1. ibid., pp. 88, 89. 2. ibid., p. 90. 3. ibid., p. 112.

which often arise from a partial knowledge of circumstances, of the mistakes which people of high pretensions to judgement are for ever falling into; and not very well pleased with her brother for imagining her blind and ignorant, and in want of counsel. He said no more.[1]

This is a marvellous piece of anticipatory dramatic irony; and, appropriately enough, it occurs on the very morning of the fateful party at the Westons'.

Harriet has a cold and cannot go, so Emma has tried to persuade Mr Elton not to attend either: she is certain he will be too concerned about Harriet ever to enjoy himself. But, to Emma's surprise, and against her wishes, he does attend – and here, for the first time, she gets an intimation of the actual state of affairs. He sits beside her after dinner, and she is somewhat relieved when he begins chattering about poor Harriet's sore throat:

But at last there seemed a perverse turn; it seemed all at once as if he were more afraid of its being a bad sore throat on her account, than on Harriet's – more anxious that she should escape the infection, than that there should be no infection in the complaint. . . . [etc.] [2]

And now, her suspicions having been aroused, Emma is somewhat distressed to find that she will ride home alone with him in the second carriage.

To restrain him as much as might be, by her own manners, she was immediately preparing to speak with exquisite calmness and gravity of the weather and the night; but scarcely had she begun, scarcely had they passed the sweep-gate and joined the other carriage, than she found her subject cut up – her hand seized – her attention demanded, and Mr Elton actually making violent love to her; availing himself of the precious opportunity, declaring sentiments which must be already well known, hoping – fearing – adoring – ready to die if she refused him; but flattering himself that his ardent attachment and unequalled love and unexampled passion could not fail of having some effect, and in short, very much resolved on being seriously accepted as soon as possible. It was

1. *Emma*, p. 112. 2. ibid., p. 124.

really so. Without scruple – without apology – without much apparent diffidence, Mr Elton, the lover of Harriet, was professing himself *her* lover.[1]

She replies that she will be glad to deliver any messages to Miss Smith: for though the truth is now plain to her, it is too enormous for ingestion. Mr Elton insists, however: '"Every thing that I have said or done, for many weeks past, has been with the sole view of marking my adoration of yourself. You cannot really, seriously, doubt it."'[2]

So occurs the dénouement of the first movement of the story – and it leaves Emma stunned, Mr Elton mortified, Harriet deeply hurt. But Emma alone, among the principals in this series of events, has learned something:

> The first error and the worst lay at her door. It was foolish, it was wrong, to take so active a part in bringing any two people together. It was adventuring too far, assuming too much, making light of what ought to be serious, a trick of what ought to be simple. She was quite concerned and ashamed, and resolved to do such things no more.[3]

But though progress has been made in the direction of self-knowledge, Emma is certainly not yet sufficiently self-aware; for in a very short time, pondering Harriet's disappointment, she resolves that 'Where the wound had been given, there must the cure be found if anywhere; and Emma felt that, till she saw her in the way of cure, there could be no true peace for herself.'[4] In other words, she still means to find Harriet a husband, but she will no longer be so 'active' or 'tricky' in her schemes of promotion. The lesson, therefore, has not penetrated Emma very deeply. Still, in the next section of the novel, she will be more careful, and (as she herself does not yet know) more personally involved. She has ignored Mr Elton's character entirely; she must acknowledge Frank Churchill's.

Beginning with the second volume, the story takes on two additional, and significant, dimensions: these are owing to the

1. ibid., p. 129.
2. ibid., p. 131.
3. ibid., pp. 136, 137.
4. ibid., p. 143.

persons of Jane Fairfax and Frank Churchill. The character of Mr Elton has not yet been completely disclosed; Emma has allowed herself the luxury of reflecting but little upon it – and we are soon to know a great deal more about him, as he is removed from the centre of her match-making schemes. Meanwhile, Frank Churchill – who is repeatedly mentioned in the first volume – appears on the scene in some completeness; Jane Fairfax appears as well, also in the round.

The predominating impressions gained of Mr Elton thus far have been that he is an excessively polite young man, with rather too fluent company manners, and a desire to marry well. Of Frank Churchill we learn, in advance of his appearance, his family relationships, and of a certain lack of resolution and independence (so Mr Knightley alleges) which prevents him from visiting his new 'mother-in-law' (that is, his step-mother), Mrs Weston. We know ahead of time as much about the second young man as we have known thus far about the first.

And Jane Fairfax presents a challenge to Emma of which Harriet has never been capable : Jane is a rival in everything except birth and prospects (including wealth). Emma dislikes her:

> Why she did not like Jane Fairfax might be a difficult question to answer; Mr Knightley had once told her it was because she saw in her the really accomplished young woman, which she wanted to be thought herself; and though the accusation had been eagerly refuted at the time, there were moments of self-examination in which her conscience could not quite acquit her.[1]

When Jane does arrive in Highbury, Emma resolves to like her; but then she finds that the new-comer, besides being beautiful and elegant, is reserved – 'she seemed determined to hazard nothing', not even about Frank Churchill (with whom she has

1. *Emma*, p. 166. 'There are ... few finer examples in fiction of suggestive reticence than Jane Austen's treatment of Jane Fairfax. The mystery of the story demands that we should be kept in the dark about her; yet we feel that we know her as well as any character that Jane Austen created.' Harold Child, 'Jane Austen', *Cambridge History of English Literature*, XII, p. 267.

previously been acquainted at Weymouth) – and 'Emma could not forgive her'.[1]

So the stage is set for a new drama, and Emma does not yet know what direction it will take. Meanwhile Miss Bates discloses, in the midst of her gratitude for a gift of Mr Woodhouse's pork, the information that Mr Elton is betrothed to a Miss Augusta Hawkins, of Bath – making perhaps the funniest remark in the book: ' "It is such a happiness when good people get together – and they always do." '[2] Emma is glad this news reaches Harriet's ear just as the latter encounters Elizabeth and Robert Martin at Ford's (the woollen-draper's), and she even encourages her friend to call upon the Martins at Abbey-Mill Farm, where old and pleasant memories are revived. Afterwards, Emma reflects:

> She would have given a great deal, or endured a great deal, to have had the Martins in a higher rank of life. They were so deserving, that a *little* higher should have been enough: but as it was, how could she have done otherwise? – Impossible! – She could not repent.[3]

The traces of uncertainty here leave the door open for future persuasion of the Martins' worthiness; at the same time Emma's present, and no doubt inevitable, opinion gives her free rein to match-make at will in the following pages.

She is prepared to like Frank Churchill and she does, both because of his kind attentions to the Westons (and to herself), and because of his apparent dislike for Jane Fairfax, whose ' "deplorable want of complexion" ' and ' "repulsive" ' reserve he berates.[4] That Emma is nearly completely wrong about him makes for one of the major ironies in the book. The entire pattern of his behaviour while at Highbury is a camouflage by which Emma, who preens herself on her own penetration, is completely taken in. Not that she is not warned: Mr Knightley sees through his major piece of deception; but she dismisses the former's protests – and even resolves to overlook

1. ibid., p. 169. 2. ibid., p. 175. 3. ibid., p. 187.
4. ibid., pp. 199 and 203 respectively.

the 'foppery and nonsense' of the young man's journey to London to get his hair cut.

The famous party at the Coles' discloses Emma at the penultimate height of her self-confidence (the ultimate will be the picnic at Box Hill). Here she is led to believe that the piano which has recently arrived for Jane Fairfax is the present of Mr Dixon, the husband of Miss Campbell, her protector's daughter. She is quite convinced that Frank cannot like Jane Fairfax much, from his behaviour to her and remarks about her. These deceptions practised on Emma are intentional and artful; it is impossible to blame her for being deceived, at this point anyway – except that she wants to believe what she does. But that she is still the victim of her own myopia is demonstrated by her reaction to Mrs Weston's suggestion that Mr Knightley may have a more than ordinary interest in Jane Fairfax:

> 'Mr Knightley and Jane Fairfax!' exclaimed Emma. 'Dear Mrs Weston, how could you think of such a thing? – Mr Knightley! – Mr Knightley must not marry! – You would not have little Henry cut out from Donwell? – Oh! no, no, Henry must have Donwell. I cannot at all consent to Mr Knightley's marrying; and I am sure it is not at all likely. I am amazed that you should think of such a thing.' [1]

She continues to object, and one of her protestations is, ' "My dear Mrs Weston, do not take to match-making. You do it very ill. Jane Fairfax mistress of the Abbey! – Oh! no, no; – every feeling revolts. For his own sake, I would not have him do so mad a thing." ' [2] To accuse her accuser of the crime of which she herself is guilty is of course transparently ironic and (with regard to her attitude to Mr Knightley) this shows the depth of Emma's self-deception.

But she has not yet fixed on a match between Frank Churchill and Harriet Smith: she is as yet too interested herself; she is even spurred to some self-examination. For, the day after the Coles' party, she is 'not quite easy' on two

1. *Emma*, p. 224. 2. ibid., p. 225.

points: first, she wonders whether 'she had not transgressed the duty of woman by woman, in betraying her suspicions of Jane Fairfax's feelings to Frank Churchill',[1] and second, she wishes she could play and sing as well as Jane. As to the first point, she has been led astray; still, in the first volume, she never, until after Mr Elton's declaration, has any scruples about her duty to Harriet; and too, her haphazardly dilatory style of drawing, her leaving everything unfinished, have given her no uneasiness. There is, of course, a difference between trying to make a match between Harriet and Mr Elton, and suggesting that Jane Fairfax is in love with a married man; there is also the fact that Emma's lack of skill in drawing might have given her uneasiness if she had to contrast it with the greater skill of another – as she had her music: in this second volume, the relationships are more complex and of greater consequence; and Emma, for the first time, has a competitor.

In the next two weeks, Emma continues to take pleasure in Frank Churchill's company, and enters spiritedly into the plans for a dance at the Crown Inn. When he is recalled to Enscombe (the Yorkshire home of his foster-parents) before the dance can take place, she reflects on the happy memories of his visit to Highbury, and:

> To complete every other recommendation, he had *almost* told her that he loved her . . . at present she could not doubt his having a decidedly warm admiration, a conscious preference of herself; and this persuasion, joined to all the rest, made her think that she *must* be a little in love with him, in spite of every previous determination against it.[2]

But Emma, however vain and however blind, is neither stupid nor unanalytical. She cannot be quite satisfied with her first appraisal of the situation.

> Emma continued to entertain no doubt of her being in love. Her ideas only varied as to the how much . . . [Yet] the conclusion of every imaginary declaration on his side was that she *refused*

1. ibid., p. 231. 2. ibid., p. 262.

him. Their affection was always to subside into friendship. Everything tender and charming was to make their parting; but still they were to part. When she became sensible of this, it struck her that she could not be very much in love, for in spite of her previous and fixed determination never to quit her father, never to marry, a strong attachment certainly must produce more of a struggle than she could foresee in her own feelings.[1]

So her match-making eyes shift to Harriet, now flustered and unhappy as the wedding day of Mr Elton approaches. For the first time, Emma thinks that an attachment between Frank Churchill and Harriet might be desirable (absence has given her some perspective on her own feelings to him) and – again for the first time – she gains an insight into one of her major failings: time and experience have given her some proportion, some self-knowledge.

'There is no charm equal to tenderness of heart,' said she ... to herself. 'There is nothing to be compared to it. Warmth and tenderness of heart, with an affectionate, open manner, will beat all the clearness of head in the world, for attraction. I am sure it will. It is tenderness of heart which makes my dear father so generally beloved – which gives Isabella all her popularity. – I have it not – but I know how to prize and respect it. – Harriet is my superior in all the charm and all the felicity it gives. Dear Harriet! – I would not change you for the clearest-headed, longest-sighted, best-judging, female breathing. Oh! the coldness of a Jane Fairfax! Harriet is worth a hundred such. – And for a wife – a sensible man's wife – it is invaluable. I mention no names; but happy the man who changes Emma for Harriet!' [2]

There is a real contradiction here: her heart goes out to Harriet and others, but is still closed to Jane Fairfax.

1. *Emma*, p. 264.

2. ibid., p. 269. Such a passage as the one just quoted should give pause to critics – H. W. Garrod, for example – who think that Jane Austen's 'primary concern in fiction was the manners of men, and not the human heart ...' 'Jane Austen: a Depreciation', in *Essays by Divers Hands, Being the Transactions of the Royal Society of Literature of the United Kingdom*, n.s., VIII (1928), p. 29.

Now that the idea has entered Emma's head of promoting a match between Harriet and Frank, she must have some encouragement to go ahead; and she gets it in the person of Mrs Elton, the 'pert and familiar' merchant's daughter who now appears in Highbury for the first time. This woman, the former Augusta Hawkins, surely one of the most amusing characters in the novel, occupies many pages with her boasting, her familiarity, her 'Knightleys', and her barouche-landaus. She is such a terrible woman that Emma cannot help feeling Harriet would have been a much better wife for the vicar. If Mr Elton had only been more sensible, he would have married a better woman – through Emma's own good offices.

Thus the stage is rapidly being set for the final act of the comedy. Again Emma is over-confident, again (for this is a characteristic of over-confidence) she does not ponder deeply enough the significance of such things as Jane Fairfax's daily walks to the post-office, even despite Mrs Elton's offer to send a servant, even despite the rain.

> Jane's solicitude about fetching her own letters had not escaped Emma. She had heard and seen it all; and felt some curiosity to know whether the wet walk of this morning had produced any. She suspected that it *had*; that it would not have been so resolutely encountered but in full expectation of hearing from some one very dear, and that it had not been in vain. She thought there was an air of greater happiness than usual – a glow both of complexion and spirits.[1]

Emma jumps to the conclusion that Mr Dixon is the author of the letters which Jane is receiving, quite ignoring Jane's own good character, blandly accepting Frank Churchill's encouragement in this belief. Frank has but to arrive again, and Emma will once more direct a drama with her own plot, the same heroine – but with a new hero, and an unexpected conclusion.

Emma, then, has reverted to something like the same state of mind that she was in when Harriet became her protégée in the first volume. There are now, however, two important

1. ibid., p. 298.

differences. She has learned enough not to be so crudely interfering in her efforts to match-make; and she has become aware – though as yet but dimly – that she cannot remove herself from association with those whose lives she would arrange. So, at the beginning of the third volume, Emma feels some apprehension at the news of Frank Churchill's arrival – more on his account than on her own:

> She wished she might be able to keep him from an absolute declaration. That would be so very painful a conclusion of their present acquaintance! – and yet, she could not help rather anticipating something decisive. She felt as if the spring would not pass without bringing a crisis, an event, a something to alter her present composed and tranquil state.[1]

A crisis will come: but it will be one largely of her own devising, and contrary to every expectation.

The long-delayed ball at the Crown Inn is the occasion for two significant developments. In the first place, Emma begins (though very slowly) to awaken to the physical charms of Mr Knightley: 'His tall, firm, upright figure ... was such as Emma felt must draw every body's eyes. ...'[2] In the second, Mr Knightley, to compensate for Mr Elton's snub of Harriet, dances with the girl, and afterwards praises her to Emma.

But Emma has little time to ponder the meaning of these events, for on the next day Harriet is frightened by some gypsies and is rescued by Frank Churchill. Certainly romance would ensue; but Emma makes a resolution:

> Everything was to take its natural course, however, neither impelled nor assisted. She would not stir a step, nor drop a hint. No, she had had enough of interference. There could be no harm in a scheme, a mere passive scheme. It was no more than a wish. Beyond it she would on no account proceed.[3]

Harriet soon confides in Emma that she will never marry, for the man in whom she is interested is so much above her:

> 'I am not at all surprised at you, Harriet. The service he rendered you was enough to warm your heart.'

1. *Emma*, p. 315. 2. ibid., p. 326. 3. ibid., p. 335.

'Service! oh! It was such an inexpressible obligation! – The very recollection of it, and all that I felt at the time – when I saw him coming – his noble look – and my wretchedness before. Such a change! In one moment such a change! From perfect misery to perfect happiness.' [1]

Harriet, as we shall much later find, is referring to Mr Knightley's gallantry at the ball; while Emma believes she is alluding to Frank Churchill and the gypsy episode. Emma now says that the matter must not be discussed ever again, and that no name should be mentioned. Thus the preparation is being made for a grand disillusionment later in the story. It is particularly ironic that Emma should be the creator of this illusion on the grounds of non-interference. Were she as curious and meddling as in the first volume, she could not now be deceived. But her resolution not to interfere in the lives of others has been but partially realized, and she will have to pay an even greater price this time.

In the following chapter (III, V), the point of view of the book changes abruptly. We grasp, through Mr Knightley's eyes, a suspicion that Frank Churchill has 'some inclination to trifle with Jane Fairfax'.[2] Emma is not privy to this suspicion; she is, however, present when Frank asks Mrs Weston the latest news about '"Mr Perry's plan of setting up his carriage"', information which could only have come from someone at the Bateses' household. And Emma chooses to ignore this piece of evidence. Indeed, when Mr Knightley confides his apprehensions to her, she replies that Frank Churchill and Miss Fairfax are

1. ibid., p. 342.

2. ibid., p. 343. This is the second time the point of view totally excludes Emma: for the first time see pp. 38, 39. Even Dr Chapman nods when he says: 'Those who have read and re-read *Emma* with the closest attention agree that never once does Miss Austen yield to the temptation of what the author of *The Awkward Age* called "going behind". The drama unfolds itself, but there are no notes, and hardly a stage direction. Even when she seems to speak in her own person she is really interpreting, not explaining, her heroine.' [R. W. Chapman], 'Jane Austen's Methods', *Times Literary Supplement* (9 February 1922), p. 82.

'... as far from any attachment or admiration for one another, as any two beings in the world can be. That is, I *presume* it to be so on her side, and I can *answer* for its being so on his. I will answer for the gentleman's indifference.'

She spoke with a confidence which staggered, with a satisfaction which silenced, Mr Knightley.[1]

Now come the high points in the novel, the excursions to Donwell and to Box Hill. Quite aside from their comic significance, which is great, they do much to hasten matters toward the final denouement. Several things happen at the first party which bear directly on Emma's present thinking. First, she sees Harriet and Mr Knightley walking *tête-à-tête* down an avenue of limes – and now she is pleased, though this scene will return to haunt her. Second, Frank Churchill, who arrives late and stays only briefly, is so agitated and 'out of humour' that she with real finality congratulates herself she is no longer in love with him – though ' "Harriet's sweet easy temper will not mind ..." '.[2] Thus Emma withdraws completely from any involvement with him, and so places herself in the same relation to him that she has previously to Mr Elton. Furthermore, for the first time she feels a warm sympathy for Jane Fairfax, beleaguered by Mrs Elton's insistence upon finding her a job as a governess. Emma's 'tenderness of heart', always incipient and intellectually desired, now begins to manifest itself spontaneously.

But this last receives a set-back the following day at Box Hill, where Emma flirts outrageously with Frank Churchill: 'Not that Emma was gay and thoughtless from any real felicity; it was rather because she felt less happy than she had expected. She laughed because she was disappointed. ...'[3] Furthermore, she is gratuitously cruel to Miss Bates, and so elicits from Mr Knightley a stern and strong remonstrance. Emma is at last deeply touched.

Never had she felt so agitated, mortified, grieved, at any circumstance in her life. She was most forcibly struck. The truth of his

1. *Emma*, p. 351. 2. ibid., p. 364. 3. ibid., p. 368.

representation there was no denying. She felt it at her heart. How could she have been so brutal, so cruel to Miss Bates! – How could she have exposed herself to such ill opinion in any one she valued! And how suffer him to leave her without saying one word of gratitude, of concurrence, of common kindness!

Time did not compose her. As she reflected more, she seemed but to feel it more. She never had been so depressed. Happily it was not necessary to speak. There was only Harriet, who seemed not in spirits herself, fagged, and very willing to be silent; and Emma felt the tears running down her cheeks almost all the way home, without being at any trouble to check them, extraordinary as they were.[1]

Henceforth, Emma does act with true tenderness of heart. She calls on Miss Bates. She tries – though for a long time unsuccessfully – to make amends to Jane Fairfax. She is kinder than ever to Mr Woodhouse. But again her self-knowledge comes too late – or very nearly; and the play, in which she has acted as director, must be played out; she must learn how little control she has actually had over those to whom she would be God.

Her first shock comes at the news of the betrothal of Frank Churchill to Jane Fairfax, an engagement of long standing; she has been thoroughly gulled by Frank Churchill. Next she finds that the superior person with whom Harriet is in love is not Frank Churchill but Mr Knightley: Emma has taught her friend to hope for a match which previously the latter never aspired to. And now – at long last – Emma realizes 'that Mr Knightley must marry no one but herself'.[2]

Emma looks deeply into her own heart, and is miserable:

To understand, thoroughly understand, her own heart was the first endeavour. To that point went every leisure moment which

1. ibid., p. 376. As Bradley points out: 'She has a generous nature. She is self-confident, and she likes to be first; but she is not vain. She is faultless in her relations with her father; and, though she will not take advice from Knightley, her readiness to take reproof and to make amends for her errors is more than magnanimous.' A. C. Bradley, 'Jane Austen', in *Essays and Studies by Members of the English Association*, II (1911), p. 23.

2. *Emma*, p. 408.

her father's claims on her allowed, and every moment of involuntary absence of mind....

She saw that there never had been a time when she did not consider Mr Knightley as infinitely the superior, or when his regard for her had not been infinitely the most dear. She saw, that in persuading herself, in fancying, in acting to the contrary, she had been entirely under a delusion, totally ignorant of her own heart – and, in short, that she had never really cared for Frank Churchill at all!

With insufferable vanity had she believed herself in the secret of everybody's feelings; with unpardonable arrogance proposed to arrange everybody's destiny. She was proved to have been universally mistaken; and she had not quite done nothing – for she had done mischief. She had brought evil on Harriet, on herself, and she too much feared, on Mr Knightley....[1]

The book ends happily, however, as happily as anyone could wish. But the outcome hardly cancels what has gone before: Emma has paid for her delusive self-confidence by truly painful humiliations. Throughout the book we have loved her for the contradictions in her nature: they are amusing; they are deeply human. The new Emma, the Emma who stands self-revealed, is perhaps no less human – and only slightly less amusing – but she is more resolved, more composed, more serene.

George Knightley and Frank Churchill

It is almost improper to say that *Emma* contains a villain: Frank Churchill is devious, hypocritical, 'slyding of corage', and occasionally quite unkind; but he seduces no innocent young girl, elopes with no scatter-brained matron, neglects no indigent widow, betrays no monstrous dishonesty. He is a villain only by contrast with the excellent Mr Knightley, whose manly vigour and forthrightness are the outward and visible signs of a sterling integrity and an (almost) unfailing sympathy.

Mr Knightley is 'a sensible man': he appraises coolly, he judges calmly, he acts decisively. But he does not do so at the

1. *Emma*, pp. 412, 413.

cost of removing himself from personal involvement with those people who make up his immediate society. For, as Emma perceives, his disdain for Frank Churchill ('"He is a person I never think of from one month's end to another..."') is excessive:

> To take a dislike to a young man, only because he appeared to be of a different disposition from himself, was unworthy the real liberality of mind which she was always used to acknowledge in him; for with all the high opinion of himself, which she had often laid to his charge, she had never before for a moment supposed it could make him unjust to the merit of another.[1]

And later, if not at this moment, it is evident that his refusal to attribute much merit to Frank Churchill is based partly on jealousy. Furthermore, his lack of enthusiasm for the ball at the Crown Inn can be attributed, retrospectively at least, to his wish that Emma should not be given too much opportunity to fall in love with Frank Churchill. But neither of these facts vitiates his basic common sense, the man-in-the-street variety which carries one very far indeed, but which hardly accounts, in Austenian terms, for all of life's dimensions, perplexities, and excitements.

He is, however, truly sensible. Consider the significance of the latter part of the first chapter, in which Emma takes credit for having made the match of Miss Taylor and Mr Weston, which Mr Woodhouse ascribes to his daughter.[2] But Mr Knightley, 'one of the few people who could see faults in Emma Woodhouse, and the only one who ever told her of them',[3] tries unsuccessfully to dampen her vanity by telling her the truth of the situation.

> 'I do not understand what you mean by "success";' said Mr Knightley. 'Success supposes endeavour. Your time has been properly and delicately spent, if you have been endeavouring for the last four years to bring about this marriage. A worthy employment

1. ibid., pp. 150, 151.
2. A. C. Bradley says that Mr Woodhouse 'is, next to Don Quixote, perhaps the most perfect gentleman in fiction ...', op. cit., p. 21.
3. *Emma*, p. 11.

for a young lady's mind! But if, which I rather imagine, your making the match, as you call it, means only your planning it, your saying to yourself one idle day, "I think it would be a very good thing for Miss Taylor if Mr Weston were to marry her," and saying it again to yourself every now and then afterwards, – why do you talk of success? Where is your merit? – what are you proud of? – you made a lucky guess; and *that* is all that can be said.' [1]

But, undepressed in her enthusiasm, she goes on to say that she will find a wife for Mr Elton; to which Mr Knightley replies that the vicar should be allowed '"to chuse his own wife"'. The fact that Emma ignores Mr Knightley's advice is significant by itself in showing that there are forces always at war with ordinary good sense; subsequent events vindicate Mr Knightley's judgement, but hardly diminish Emma's stature.

Emma and Mr Knightley are clearly and openly at odds with one another in their respective choices for Harriet Smith's hand in marriage. Emma chooses Mr Elton for her, and does all within her power to effect a match; Robert Martin, having chosen Harriet, consults Mr Knightley and is given the latter's blessing. Emma is misled by her desire to run things: she thinks she is having much success; Mr Knightley, motivated by a cool judgement not only of Mr Elton's ambition but of Robert Martin's worth and Harriet's real position, would bring his yeoman and Mrs Goddard's boarder together. It is all Emma's fault that Mr Knightley's choice is not made at once – as it *is* made, ironically, in the final section of the novel, this time to Emma's intense pleasure.

But Mr Knightley possesses other attributes besides that of common sense. Deep within him is a respect for the established social order, as is shown in his approval of Robert Martin's application for Harriet Smith's hand in marriage. Martin, a simple farmer, is capable and conscientious – only just a gentleman. Harriet, however, 'the natural daughter of somebody', is good enough for him – or almost; for, as she is illegitimate, and a rather silly girl, he is '"as much her superior

1. *Emma*, pp. 12, 13.

in sense as in situation"', in Mr Knightley's own words. Furthermore, his deference to Mr Woodhouse, despite the latter's eternal preoccupation with health and food, is based in part at least upon the respect due from one gentleman to another. And finally, it is inconceivable to think that Mr Knightley would marry beneath himself.

He is, however, not by any means phlegmatic in his social attitudes. For he cannot be blind to the pretensions of Mrs Elton, though it may be argued that as she belongs to the ranks of the *nouveaux riches*, she may not be worthy of consideration in conventional terms. But certainly she is more genteel by birth than Harriet Smith; yet Mr Knightley prefers the latter.

'... I will do you the justice to say [he tells Emma], that you would have chosen for him better than he has chosen for himself. – Harriet Smith has some first-rate qualities, which Mrs Elton is totally without. An unpretending, single-minded artless girl – infinitely to be preferred by any man of sense and taste to such a woman as Mrs Elton.' [1]

Propriety is another of his attributes. It is easy for Emma to think Miss Bates a silly woman; at one point (the picnic at Box Hill), it is even easy for her to make rather cruel fun of the woman. But Mr Knightley, whose clear-sightedness has never blinded him to Miss Bates's faults, nevertheless treats her with unfailing kindness, and sternly berates Emma for the Box Hill episode.

Sensible, proper, kind, open, and vigorous – these are the words which come most readily to mind to describe George Knightley. But what would have happened had his advice been followed, his views been attended to? Emma would not have made a match for Mr Elton; Harriet would have married Mr Martin at once; Frank Churchill would not have been made so much of by Emma, and so forth: in short, the book could not have existed. Are we then to suppose that Emma is meant merely to exhibit the foibles of the world against a constant standard of values exemplified by Mr Knightley? Not at all:

1. ibid., p. 331.

for then we should have seen him as the central figure, and the novel would have been a didactic treatise. Instead, Emma Woodhouse is the centre of attention and attraction. Cleverness, charm, subtlety, wit, receptivity – these are often in conflict with what Mr Knightley represents. But though contradictory, they are as thoroughly beloved by the author as the less exciting ingredients in Mr Knightley's philosophy. Yet, as Dr Chapman says, 'all must agree that he is a perfect English gentleman . . .' [1]

From the first mention of Frank Churchill there is a hint of dash and flair about him – he is a fashionable youth, and surrounded with mystery.

> Mr Frank Churchill was one of the boasts of Highbury, and a lively curiosity to see him prevailed, though the compliment was so little returned that he had never been there in his life. His coming to visit his father had been often talked of but never achieved.[2]

Here is the first suggestion of his basic faults – selfishness, and want of consideration: though Emma, and perhaps the reader, are put off by the dutiful and 'highly prized letter' to Miss Taylor on her marriage to his father. But when Frank Churchill does not come to Highbury, Mr Knightley (in his usual role of *raisonneur*) complains of the young man's lack of resolution and inattention to duty. ' "There is one thing, Emma, which a man can always do, if he chuses, and that is, his duty; not by manoeuvring and finessing, but by vigour and resolution." ' [3]

Before Frank's arrival in Hartfield, therefore, we know the direction in which his faults will lie. In the first volume, he has been dangled before us as a person to watch. He is interesting. When at last he does make his appearance in the second volume, we (and Emma) are prepared for any slip which will disclose the true Frank Churchill.

But his whole manner seems to give the lie to advance expectations. He is entirely pleasing, not only to the Westons

1. *Jane Austen Facts and Problems*, p. 201. 2. *Emma*, p. 17.
3. ibid., p. 146.

and the Woodhouses, but in his attitude to Highbury and Hartfield.

> Emma watched and decided, that with such feelings as were now shewn, it could not be fairly supposed that he had been ever voluntarily absenting himself; that he had not been acting a part, or making a parade of insincere professions; and that Mr Knightley certainly had not done him justice.[1]

Yet it is not long before chinks begin to appear in the armour of his personality. First, he makes some unpleasant remarks about Jane Fairfax – speaks of her '"most deplorable want of complexion"', and her '"repulsive"' quality of reserve: '"There is safety in reserve, but no attraction. One cannot love a reserved person."'[2] His purpose in making these remarks is to deceive Emma – but we do not yet know this; we only know that he is exhibiting bad taste. Second, he goes to London for the sole purpose of getting his hair cut. This is a piece of frivolity, of wanton lightness, which even Emma can recognize – 'there was an air of foppery and nonsense in it which she could not approve.'[3] Still, she is willing to overlook this fault, and to enter enthusiastically into his schemes.

But it is not till the third volume that we discover the extent of his deception – his secret engagement to Jane Fairfax, which quite stuns Emma. Yet Frank is not a wicked man; his deceits have not amounted to much, and it is probably true, as Mr Knightley says, that he will become greatly improved as the husband of Jane Fairfax.

6. PERSUASION

Anne Elliot

'There are those', Louis Kronenberger reminds us, 'who think Jane Austen tea-tablish, as there are those who think

1. ibid., p. 197.
2. ibid., pp. 199 and 203 respectively.
3. ibid., p. 205.

that Mozart tinkles.' [1] 'Those' have never read *Persuasion*, a sad love story with a happy ending. Here, more clearly and more sweetly than in any of the other novels, is exposed the conflict between two schemes of values: those of prudence, and those of love. Anne Elliot contains both and the result is a contradiction which causes nearly a decade of unhappiness to her; her reconciliation with Captain Wentworth stems not from the resolution of these opposites, but from a series of fortuitous circumstances which makes the match possible after all. Never, even at the end of the book, can she abandon her commitment to the prudential values, even when she is happily betrothed to Captain Wentworth. Yet she is a complete, a fully human, heroine. John Bailey writes: 'There are few heroines in fiction whom we love so much, feel for so much, as we love and feel for Anne Elliot.' [2]

Anne Elliot is twenty-seven years old when the book opens and 'with an elegance of mind and sweetness of character, which must have placed her high with any people of real understanding, was nobody with either father or sister: her word had no weight; her convenience was always to give way; – she was only Anne.' [3] At first we see her as the only sensible member of her family, advising a programme of retrenchment which will permit the Elliots to continue at Kellynch Hall, despite financial difficulties – but strenuously opposed by her father, who then takes his lawyer's advice to let Kellynch and move to Bath. It is only when the estate is leased, to an Admiral Croft and his wife, that we learn of Anne's other dimension: for Mrs Croft is the sister of a Frederick Wentworth, who

> had come into Somersetshire, in the summer of 1806 [when Anne was nineteen]; and having no parent living, found a home for half a year, at Monkford. He was, at that time, a remarkably fine young man, with a great deal of intelligence, spirit and brilliancy;

1. In his introduction to the Harper's Modern Classics edition of *Pride and Prejudice*, New York, 1950, p. xi.

2. *Introductions to Jane Austen*, London, 1931, p. 94.

3. *Persuasion*, p.5.

and Anne an extremely pretty girl, with gentleness, modesty, taste, and feeling. – Half the sum of attraction, on either side, might have been enough, for he had nothing to do, and she had hardly anybody to love; but the encounter of such lavish recommendations could not fail. They were gradually acquainted, and when acquainted, rapidly and deeply in love. It would be difficult to say which had seen highest perfection in the other, or which had been the happiest; she, in receiving his declarations and proposals, or he in having them accepted.[1]

But Sir Walter and Lady Russell both disapproved the match: Commander Wentworth was young, not rich, and in 'a most uncertain profession': the Navy. Though he was confident, though he was brilliant, Lady Russell 'deprecated the connexion in every light'; and Anne was 'persuaded to believe the engagement a wrong thing – indiscreet, improper, hardly capable of success, and not deserving it'.[2] This was the beginning, though not the end, of Anne Elliot's difficulty. She has never been able to forget Frederick Wentworth – nor could her prudence dictate a marriage to Charles Musgrove when she was twenty-two – three years later. Now, at twenty-seven, she is no more able to forget her first attachment.

Luckily, she stays behind at Uppercross Cottage with her sister Mary Musgrove and family, when Sir Walter and Elizabeth (accompanied by the egregious Mrs Clay) go to Bath. And Frederick Wentworth does come to Kellynch Hall to visit the Crofts: but, having felt himself misused by Anne eight years before, it is natural that his meeting with her should be awkward and cool. He bows, she curtseys: that is all; and then she hears from Mary that Captain Wentworth thinks her ' "altered beyond his knowledge" '.

He had thought her wretchedly altered, and, in the first moment of appeal, had spoken as he felt. He had not forgiven Anne Elliot. She had used him ill; deserted and disappointed him; and worse, she had shown a feebleness of character in doing so which his own decided, confident temper could not endure. She had given

1. ibid., p. 26. 2. ibid., p. 27.

him up to oblige others. It had been the effect of over-persuasion. It had been weakness and timidity.[1]

The remainder of the novel, however, concerns itself with the reconstitution of an alliance which over-persuasion has put asunder. No reader can be in doubt, however, as to the final outcome; but, as the essence of suspense is waiting for the expected, the succeeding chapters are read with mounting interest – for we wonder how the lovers will, at last, be reunited. There are many difficulties to be overcome, the first of which is Captain Wentworth's deliberate lack of interest in Anne; the second his evident desire to marry – and probably one of the Miss Musgroves; the third, the red herring in the person of William Walter Elliot, heir to Kellynch.

In the natural course of events, Anne and Captain Wentworth must see a good deal of each other; they meet frequently at Uppercross Great House, where he goes to see the Miss Musgroves, and she because it is the home of Mary's parents-in-law; they meet also at Uppercross Cottage, because Charles Musgrove and Wentworth often go shooting together. All, however, is excessively formal and distant. To Anne, 'his cold politeness, his ceremonious grace, were worse than any thing'.[2] And she is galled by his warmth and gaiety of attitude towards both the Musgrove girls, though she is unable to tell which of them he prefers. She is surprised, agitated, and pleased when one day he quietly and unexpectedly removes little Charles Musgrove from her back;[3] but this incident cannot make her reflect that his attitude towards her is softening. On the other hand, she soon gets more comprehensive evidence that he cannot forgive her defection.

This comes when she overhears Captain Wentworth and Louisa Musgrove talking behind a hedgerow:

1. *Persuasion*, p. 61. 2. ibid., p. 72.

3. 'Don't you see,' writes Maria Edgeworth, 'Captain Wentworth, or rather don't you in her place feel him, taking the boisterous child off her back as she kneels by the sick boy on the sofa?' A. J. C. Hare, ed., *The Life and Letters of Maria Edgeworth*, Boston, 1895, I, p. 260 (to Mrs Ruxton, 21 February 1818).

'Your sister [he says] is an amiable creature; but *yours* is the character of decision and firmness, I see. If you value her conduct or happiness, infuse as much of your own spirit into her, as you can. But this, no doubt, you have been always doing. It is the worst evil of too yielding and indecisive character, that no influence over it can be depended on. – You are never sure of a good impression being durable. Every body may sway it; let those who would be happy be firm.' [1]

Anne feels that this conversation should be taken as a rebuke to herself. It now also seems clear that Louisa is the girl of his choice, an idea that gains weight as a reconciliation between Henrietta Musgrove and Charles Hayter takes place soon thereafter. To cap it all, she is present at a conversation between Admiral and Mrs Croft during which the former states with some assurance that Frederick will certainly marry one of the Musgrove girls.

So all seems settled; at least it seems certain that Captain Wentworth has determined to forget Anne Elliot, and is succeeding in doing so. Then comes the journey to Lyme, where she meets Captain Wentworth's friends, the Harvilles, and the recently bereaved Captain Benwick, whose grief, ironically, she helps to alleviate.

When the evening was over, Anne could not but be amused at the idea of her coming to Lyme, to preach patience and resignation to a young man whom she had never seen before; nor could she help fearing, on more serious reflection, that, like many other great moralists and preachers, she had been eloquent on a point in which her own conduct would ill bear examination.[2]

This, however, is not the climax of the visit – only a commentary on Anne's state of mind. The climax comes on the final walk which the party takes before leaving the watering place.

There was too much wind to make the high part of the new Cobb pleasant for the ladies, and they agreed to get down the steps to the lower, and all were contented to pass quietly and carefully down the steep flight, excepting Louisa; she must be jumped down

1. ibid., p. 88. 2. ibid., p. 101.

them by Captain Wentworth. In all their walks, he had had to jump her from the stiles; the sensation was delightful to her. The hardness of the pavement for her feet, made him less willing upon the present occasion; he did it, however; she was safely down, and instantly, to shew her enjoyment, ran up the steps to be jumped down again. He advised her against it, thought the jar too great; but no, he reasoned and talked in vain; she smiled and said, 'I am determined I will': he put out his hands; she was too precipitate by half a second, she fell on the pavement on the lower Cobb, and was taken up lifeless![1]

Everyone is too upset to think – everyone but Anne. Mary's reaction is, '"She is dead! She is dead!"' Henrietta faints, and Captain Wentworth calls for help, while Captain Benwick and Charles Musgrove stand by ineffectually. But Anne takes over: with calmness and decision, she orders Benwick and her brother-in-law to give some assistance to Wentworth; she suggests that a surgeon be fetched; and that Louisa be carried to the inn.

So ends the first volume of the novel, though Anne is not soon to learn what a profound impression her behaviour at the accident has made upon Captain Wentworth. Several days later, she is gratified to learn (from the Crofts) that he has inquired particularly after her; but any possible resurgence of hope is quashed when she learns that he is going to Shropshire to visit his brother.

Besides, she and Lady Russell go to Bath to join Sir Walter, Elizabeth, and Mrs Clay. Here there is a new interest: William Walter Elliot, for many years estranged from the rest of the family because of his marriage to a girl other than Elizabeth (which particularly enraged Sir Walter), is in Bath, a recent widower, and fully attentive to his relations. Anne has a moment of suspicion at his wishing to effect a reconciliation after so many years; but when she sees him, she is much pleased.

He was quite as good-looking as he had appeared at Lyme [where she had caught a glimpse of him], his countenance improved by

1. *Persuasion*, p. 109.

speaking, and his manners were so exactly what they ought to be, so polished, so easy, so particularly agreeable, that she could compare them in excellence to only one person's manners. They were not the same, but they were, perhaps, equally good.[1]

And this pleasure continues, even increases as she hears from Lady Russell that she has been the subject of close inquiry, and fulsome praise, by the heir to Kellynch. She enjoys toying with the idea of marrying him, and likes to think of being the future Lady Elliot of Kellynch Hall: but, after a month, she feels some hesitation:

Mr Elliot was too generally agreeable. Various as were the tempers in her father's house, he pleased them all. He endured too well, – stood too well with everybody.[2]

It is wise for the reader to pause and reflect here that Anne, who as yet knows nothing but good about Mr Elliot, rejects the possibility of marrying him, despite the prudential values inherent in such an attachment: her rejection is based on the commitment to another, and opposing, standard.

Meanwhile, Captain Wentworth arrives in Bath and encounters her with William Walter Elliot. Her former fiancé 'was obviously more struck and confused by the sight of her than she had ever observed before; he looked quite red.'[3] She too is affected, and in her own mind all the more disdains Mr Elliot, especially when Captain Wentworth begins not only to show some signs of resurgent affection, but to manifest a jealousy of the other man.

Jealousy of Mr Elliot! It was the only intelligible motive. Captain Wentworth jealous of her affection! Could she have believed it a week ago – three hours ago! For a moment the gratification was exquisite. But alas! There were very different thoughts to succeed. How was such jealousy to be quieted? How was the truth to reach him? How, in all the peculiar disadvantages of their respective situations, would he ever learn her real sentiments? It was misery to think of Mr. Elliot's attentions. – Their evil was incalculable.[4]

1. ibid., p. 143. 2. ibid., p. 161. 3. ibid., p. 175.
4. ibid., pp. 190, 191.

Then Anne learns from Mrs Smith, a former school friend and now a widow in unhappy circumstances, that William Walter Elliot is deceitful, hypocritical, dishonest. So Anne is – as far as the book's terms are concerned – now free to reject him both because the attachment would be without love and because it would be imprudent. Now the book can move quickly on to its happy denouement, although there is to be fuller clarification of the issues, on the way.

In a discussion with Captain Harville (which is overheard by Wentworth), Anne discloses her own strong commitment to a certain aspect of the system of values implied by the word love. She says (apropos of the characteristics of women as against those of men):

> 'Oh!' cried Anne eagerly, 'I hope I do justice to all that is felt by you, and by those who resemble you. God forbid that I should undervalue the warm and faithful feelings of any of my fellow-creatures. I should deserve utter contempt if I dared to suppose that true attachment and constancy were known only by woman. No, I believe you capable of every thing great and good in your married lives. I believe you equal to every important exertion, and to every domestic forbearance, so long as – if I may be allowed the expression, so long as you have an object. I mean, while the woman you love lives, and lives for you. All the privilege I claim for my own sex (it is not a very enviable one, you need not covet it) is that of loving longest, when existence or when hope is gone.' [1]

This warm and enthusiastic statement spurs Captain Wentworth at last to tender Anne a proposal of marriage; it takes but little time to effect a joyous reconciliation not only to each other – but to the rest of the family. One reason why Captain Wentworth is now acceptable is that he has fulfilled every promise which his optimistic temperament declared nine years before. Anne's judgement is now maturer and firmer than it was when she was a girl of nineteen; she could now more reasoningly disagree with Lady Russell. Nevertheless, she cannot regret her decision to take Lady Russell's advice.

1. *Persuasion*, p. 235.

'I have been thinking over the past, and trying impartially to judge of the right and wrong, I mean with regard to myself; and I must believe that I was right, much as I suffered from it, that I was perfectly right in being guided by the friend whom you will love better than you do now. To me, she was in the place of a parent. Do not mistake me, however. I am not saying that she did not err in her advice. It was, perhaps, one of those cases in which advice is good or bad only as the event decides; and for myself, I certainly never should, in any circumstance of tolerable similarity, give such advice. But I mean, that I was right in submitting to her, and that if I had done otherwise, I should have suffered more in continuing the engagement than I did even in giving it up, because I should have suffered in my conscience. I have now, as far as such a sentiment is allowable in human nature, nothing to reproach myself with; and if I mistake not, a strong sense of duty is no bad part of a woman's portion.' [1]

It is plain, then, that the ironic dilemma (which is the problem posed by the novel) is never resolved. Although, owing to many happily fortuitous circumstances, Anne Elliot and Frederick Wentworth are reunited at the end – there still exists potentially in every relationship between a man and a woman the conflict between love and prudence.

Frederick Wentworth and William Walter Elliot

Frederick Wentworth's real rival in *Persuasion* is not William Walter Elliot but over-conventionality. The heroine never forgets her first love, neither does she abandon hope; the sanguine naval officer is, like Christopher Newman in *The American*, 'a good man wronged' – and, as with James's hero, the wrongdoers are not so much competitors for the heroine's hand, but adherents to a set of standards which he cannot give subservient allegiance to. Young Mr Elliot, like Lord Deepmere, is a red herring.

When we first meet Frederick Wentworth, he is a young and promising commander, 'a remarkably fine young man, with a great deal of intelligence, spirit, and brilliancy. . . .' [2]

1. ibid., p. 246.

2. ibid., p. 26.

He is subtly uncomplicated – simple and straightforward, but clever.

Captain Wentworth had no fortune. He had been lucky in his profession, but spending freely, what had come freely, had realized nothing. But, he was confident that he should soon be rich; – full of life and ardour, he knew that he should soon have a ship, and soon be on a station that would lead to every thing he wanted. He had always been lucky; he knew he should be so still. – Such confidence, powerful in its own warmth, and bewitching in the wit which often expressed it, must have been enough for Anne; but Lady Russell saw it very differently. – His sanguine temper, and fearlessness of mind, operated very differently on her. She saw in it but an aggravation of the evil. It only added a dangerous character to himself. He was brilliant, he was headstrong. – Lady Russell had little taste for wit; and of anything approaching to imprudence a horror. She deprecated the connexion in every light.[1]

So Anne, having been persuaded not only by Lady Russell but also by Sir Walter, turns him down, and he leaves the neighbourhood, a disappointed man – to return almost eight years later with the very natural determination not to reopen the affair. He is cool to Anne. But now, having fulfilled all his early promise, he wishes to marry. As he says to his sister, only half-playfully:

'Yes, here I am, Sophia, quite ready to make a foolish match. Any body between fifteen and thirty may have me for asking. A little beauty, and a few smiles, and a few compliments to the navy, and I am a lost man. Should not this be enough for a sailor, who has had no society among women to make him nice?'[2]

He is jocose with the Miss Musgroves, whose high spirits and flattery delight him; extraordinarily kind to Mrs Musgrove, whose retrospective grief over poor Richard evokes astringent criticism from Jane Austen; but deliberately unresponsive to Anne Elliot.

Yet he cannot ignore her altogether, for in the nature of things they are thrown together a great deal, on account of

1. *Persuasion*, p. 27. 2. ibid., p. 62.

the family connexions. He is thus able to perform the small but moving act of kindness, in removing young Charles Musgrove from Anne's back. It is, however, at Lyme, that he is forced to return all of his attention and affection to his first love – when Louisa behaves so stupidly, and Anne so coolly. At Bath, very much later, we learn what he has been thinking in this period:

... he had meant to forget her, and believed it to be done. He had imagined himself indifferent, when he had only been angry; and he had been unjust to her merits, because he had been a sufferer from them ... but he was obliged to acknowledge that only at Uppercross had he learnt to do her justice, and only at Lyme had he begun to understand himself.[1]

But the reunion is gloriously happy – and as he tells Anne, '"I must endeavour to subdue my mind to my fortune. I must learn to brook being happier than I deserve."'[2]

William Walter Elliot appears first under a cloud. As heir to Kellynch, he was expected to marry Elizabeth; instead, to the mortification of Sir Walter and his eldest daughter, young Mr Elliot married 'a rich woman of inferior birth'. But, more than that, he has spoken ill of the Elliots of Kellynch Hall, and it is a severe commentary on Sir Walter, Elizabeth, and Lady Russell that he should be welcomed so readily back into their good graces when, as a personable widower, he shows up at Bath. Only Anne has some doubts:

... she had the sensation of there being something more than immediately appeared, in Mr Elliot's wishing, after an interval of so many years, to be well received by them.[3]

Yet he is courteous, attractive – altogether very pleasing. Anne, in fact, soon finds him 'too generally agreeable' to everyone; she begins to suspect his motives, though she cannot understand what they can be. But from Mrs Smith she finds out the truth about her personable young cousin – that he is in fact a heartless wretch; not a mere hypocrite but a false friend: heartless, indifferent, selfish. He has come to Bath to

1. ibid., pp. 241, 242. 2. ibid., p. 247. 3. ibid., p. 140.

keep Sir Walter from marrying Mrs Clay, and thus from the possibility of producing a male heir to Kellynch. Young Mr Elliot succeeds in that endeavour – by enticing Mrs Clay to London, out of harm's way.

Generally speaking – and to summarize this chapter in a sentence – Jane Austen's characters are instruments of a profound vision: she laughs at man, but only because she takes him seriously; examines humanity closely, but the more she perceives the less she understands – or perhaps one had better say, the more she understands, the more is she perplexed by the contradictions which she finds. She has what Vivas calls 'a conception of the total personality'. Man, he says,

> the actual actor of the moral drama, as we have come to know him through the efforts of poets and sages, is a complex, burdened, pitiful, and wonderful creature. He may be the paragon of animals, of noble reason and of infinite faculty; in action he may be like an angel and in apprehension like a god; but he is also a petulant thinking reed and a hopeless mess. He is in love with life but also hates it deeply and subtly. He is capable of crime and sin but also has a tyrannical and whimsical conscience that tortures him for trivial misdemeanours as brutally as it punishes him for unpardonable sins. Narcissistic, he hates himself; full of insufferable vanity, he seeks to humiliate himself; the victim of systematic self-deception, he is capable of unsparing self-knowledge. But, above all, in what he wants he is hopelessly confused, vague, self-deceived, inconsistent, and divided. Nothing, I suspect, would give him a worse sense of misery and of guilt than letting him have all that he wants. In any case it would take an Augustine, a Freud, a Dostoevski, a Kierkegaard, and a Shakespeare, aided by a Boas and a Machiavelli, pooling their several talents and techniques, to split open the secret heart of this contemptible lump of living clay and extract its wonderful essence.[1]

And Jane Austen makes no inconsiderable contribution in this quest.

1. Eliseo Vivas, *The Moral Life and the Ethical Life*, Chicago, 1950, p. 60.

CHAPTER IV

Styles

'THERE,' writes Jane Austen, with an almost audible sigh, 'I flatter myself I have constructed you a smartish Letter, considering my want of Materials. But like my dear Dr Johnson I beleive [*sic*] I have dealt more in Notions than Facts.' [1] And few students have failed to observe her great indebtedness to her 'dear Dr Johnson'. Indeed, in examining Jane Austen's style we must remember that, for her, Johnsonian diction and syntax are the standard. The principal significance of this fact is indicated by Miss Lascelles: 'To us Jane Austen appears like one who inherits a prosperous and well-ordered estate – the heritage of a prose style in which neither generalization nor abstraction need signify vagueness, because there was close enough agreement as to the scope and significance of such terms.' [2] Thus she can write, without the least suspicion of irony, the following remarks about John Willoughby:

> The world had made him extravagant and vain – Extravagance and vanity had made him cold-hearted and selfish. Vanity, while seeking its own guilty triumph at the expense of another, had involved him in a real attachment, which extravagance, or at least its offspring, necessity, had required to be sacrificed.[3]

That is, she can use abstractions freely, her sentences can be carefully balanced, she can employ rhetorical repetition – all, as it were, naturally: it is her tradition. And in fact it is by

1. *Letters*, I, p. 181 (to Cassandra Austen, 8 February 1807).

2. Mary Lascelles, *Jane Austen and Her Art*, p. 107. Miss Lascelles has written a most perceptive analysis of Jane Austen's style, and to it I am very heavily indebted for what appears in this chapter.

3. *Sense and Sensibility*, p. 331.

virtue of this tradition that the irony of Jane Austen's style derives much of its sharpness and point. For of course, like all great writers, she goes beyond her literary heritage – takes it, employs it, but changes it. 'To conform merely,' as Eliot points out, 'would be for the new work not really to conform at all; it would not be new, and would therefore not be a work of art.' [1] It is thus with the sense of her novelty as well as with the knowledge of her literary heritage (which of course goes beyond Johnson) that we must look at Jane Austen's style.

But here it is necessary to insert a long parenthesis, for one of the principal confusions that has gathered itself about the term 'irony' has to do with style. To the rhetoricians – and to many lexicographers – 'irony' means the stylistic technique of reversal, or at least transformation, of literal meaning. Validity, in language, depends upon what is; therefore, it is perfectly accurate to use the word 'ironic' to describe the mechanisms of rhetorical shifts. Yet, as we have already seen, it is possible to employ these techniques without being ironic in the central signification of the word: Swift, for example, simply buttresses his unambiguous moral indignation in 'A Modest Proposal', by sarcastically using language in such a manner as to require the reader to reverse its meaning. This is satire.[2] Jane Austen likewise often uses irony as a stylistic device and for quite un-ironic purposes – to flay, to poke fun, to underline a decided judgement – when there is no real contradiction involved. Thus, she wholly condemns (to incorrigible inanity) the Reverend William Collins, whose famous orotund letters are meant to be read with an eye to the unconscious ridicule which they contain. But more often these apparently plain rhetorical displays are related to the larger ironic themes of the novels themselves. We have already observed something of this relation in the chapter on point of view; now it is possible to attack the problem more directly.

1. T. S. Eliot, 'Tradition and the Individual Talent', in *Selected Essays, 1917–1932*, New York, 1932, p. 5.

2. Swift is, of course, ironic elsewhere.

Fielding, like his contemporaries and predecessors, uses the mock-heroic technique for both satirical and comic purposes. There is, for instance, this description of Mrs Waters, as she turns upon Tom Jones 'the whole artillery of love':

> First, from two lovely blue eyes, whose bright orbs flashed lightning at their discharge, flew forth two pointed ogles; but, happily for our hero, hit only a vast piece of beef which he was then conveying into his plate, and harmless spent their force. The fair warrior perceived their miscarriage, and immediately from her fair bosom drew forth a deadly sigh. A sigh which none could have heard unmoved, and which was sufficient at once to have swept off a dozen beaus; so soft, so sweet, so tender, that the insinuating air must have found its subtle way to the heart of our hero, had it not unluckily been driven from his ears by the coarse bubbling of some bottled ale, which at that time he was pouring forth. Many other weapons did she assay; but the god of eating (if there be any such deity, for I do not confidently assert it) preserved his votary; or perhaps it may not be *dignus vindice nodus*, and the present security of Jones may be accounted for by natural means; for as love frequently preserves from the attacks of hunger, so may hunger possibly, in some cases, defend us against love.[1]

The devices in this passage are not very difficult to explain. In mocking (incidentally) two aspects of the Courtly Love tradition (that love is transmitted through the eyes, and that the lover cannot eat), he employs a combination of high-flown and humble language – *orbs* against *ogles*, for instance – which forms a comic contrast; he uses a tortuous syntax to support a series of trifles. No one for a moment doubts the intent of the passage; it is very broad, very plain. Jane Austen never once employs the mock-heroic 'artillery'; she refines and subtilizes and extends the tradition. Her diction is only slightly orotund, her over-elaborate syntax never aspires to the mock-heroic. Thus, Marianne Dashwood is both the target of her comedy and, as we have seen, the subject of her irony. Marianne

1. *The History of Tom Jones, a Foundling*, New York, Modern Library, n.d., p. 435.

was *reasonable* enough to allow that a man of five and thirty might well have outlived *all* acuteness of feeling and *every* exquisite power of enjoyment. She was perfectly disposed to make *every* allowance for the colonel's *advanced* state of life which humanity required.[1]

The reader's first impression may be that it is Jane Austen who is describing Marianne as 'reasonable' here, but the very over-statement – '*all* acuteness of feeling', '*every* exquisite power' – throws such an assumption in doubt; and confirmation comes from the use of the word 'humanity', applying to the 'advanced state of life' of a man thirty-five years old. After being attracted to Willoughby:

Marianne began now to perceive that the *desperation* which had *seized* her at sixteen and a half, of ever seeing a man who could satisfy her ideas of perfection, had been rash and unjustifiable.[2]

Here, as in Fielding, is the use of language too heavy for the structure it must support – and so the diction casts the shadow of suspicion on the validity of the thought. Before Catherine Morland departs from Bath:

... the maternal anxiety of Mrs Morland will be naturally supposed to be *most severe.* A *thousand alarming presentiments of evil* to her beloved Catherine from this *terrific* separation must *oppress* her heart with sadness, and *drown her in tears.* ...[3]

Actually, we know that Mrs Morland is a sensible woman, and that she has no presentiments of any kind that her daughter will suffer from any evils at Bath, which is but a short distance away. Only addicts of the Gothic novel would find such an extravagant maternal response conventional. At the Upper Rooms, Catherine finds that:

... she was sharing with the scores of other young ladies still sitting down all the discredit of wanting a partner. To be *disgraced* in the eye of the *world,* to wear the appearance of *infamy* while

1. *Sense and Sensibility*, p. 35. Italics my own here as elsewhere in this chapter, unless otherwise noted.

2. ibid., p. 49.

3. *Northanger Abbey*, p. 18.

her heart is all *purity*, her actions all innocence, and the misconduct of another the true source of her *debasement*, is one of those circumstances which peculiarly belong to the heroine's life, and her *fortitude* under it what particularly dignifies her character.[1]

All this display of high-powered diction is occasioned by John Thorpe's failure to turn up promptly to dance with Catherine; the criticism of Gothic orotundity is of course implicit.

By the same device Jane Austen discloses her sharply critical attitude toward the Bingley sisters. Because they think Jane Bennet 'sweet'

Miss Bennet was therefore *established* as a sweet girl, and their brother felt *authorized* by such *commendation* to think of her as he chose.[2]

When Caroline Bingley writes to Jane, she says: '"If you are not so *compassionate* as to dine today with Louisa and me, we shall be in danger of *hating* each other for the rest of our lives."'[3] Behind the diction we see Caroline Bingley and Mrs Hurst as they really are – snobbish, domineering, self-consequential. And Mary Bennet's remarks are loaded with heavy words:

'While I can have my mornings to myself ... it is enough. – I think it no *sacrifice* to join occasionally in evening engagements. Society *has claims on* us all; and I *profess* myself one of those who consider intervals of *recreation and amusement* as desirable for every body.'[4]

Her sisters have only asked her to go walking to Meryton – and this is her way of saying 'yes'. Again – and perhaps even more obvious – is William Collins's proposal to Elizabeth: '"Believe me, my dear Miss Elizabeth, that your modesty, so far from doing you any *disservice*, rather adds to your other *perfections*."' Later: '"And now nothing remains for me but to assure you in the *most animated language* of the *violence* of my affection."'[5] Nor does he change. After Elizabeth has been six weeks at Hunsford, Mr Collins says to her:

1. ibid., p. 53.
2. *Pride and Prejudice*, p. 17.
3. ibid., p. 30.
4. ibid., p. 87.
5. ibid., pp. 105, 106.

'In truth I must acknowledge that, with all the disadvantages of this humble parsonage, I should not think any one abiding in it an *object of compassion*, while they are *sharers of our intimacy* at Rosings.' [1]

Very often there is but a single word which gives a hint of irony to a passage. Thus after listening to John Knightley complain about going out to an evening party in bad weather, Emma 'could not be complying, she dreaded being quarrelsome; her *heroism* reached only to silence.' [2] However, Jane Austen is not afraid, when she wishes to present a character (like William Collins) in a particularly unfavourable light, to stack heavy words together. Elizabeth Elliot, for example, 'would have *rejoiced* to be certain of being properly *solicited* by *baronet-blood* within the next *twelvemonth* or two'.[3] And here the choice of words shows us what a complete snob Miss Elliot is.

This orotundity, as contained in the passages just cited, cannot be misunderstood by the experienced reader: the contradiction between statement and meaning does not have further reference to any ambivalent intention. Marianne is plainly a moon-struck adolescent, William Collins clearly an ass – and so forth. It is only in relation to the central significance of the books themselves that such ironies take on a greater complexity. Thus it is necessary to consider the function of Mr Collins not only as the instrument of Jane Austen's ridicule, but also as the agent of Charlotte Lucas's moral collapse; and Marianne as more than the victim of sentimental delusion – as, in fact, a quite lovable human being. But this deliberately rococo use of words extends as well to syntax. She out-Johnsons Johnson. For example, there is the letter from William Collins to Mr Bennet:

The disagreement subsisting between yourself and my late honoured father always gave me much uneasiness, and since I have had the misfortune to lose him, I have frequently wished to heal the breach; but for some time I was kept back by my own

1. *Pride and Prejudice*, p. 216.
2. *Emma*, p. 114.
3. *Persuasion*, p. 7.

doubts, fearing lest it might seem disrespectful to his memory for me to be on good terms with any one, with whom it had always pleased him to be at variance. ... My mind however is now made up on the subject, for having received ordination at Easter, I have been so fortunate as to be distinguished by the patronage of the Right Honourable Lady Catherine de Bourgh, widow of Sir Lewes de Bourgh, whose bounty and beneficence has preferred me to the valuable rectory of this parish, where it shall be my earnest endeavour to demean myself with grateful respect towards her Ladyship, and be ever ready to perform those rites and ceremonies which are instituted by the Church of England [etc.].[1]

Aside from the words themselves, and particularly the clichés (which will be discussed later), the over-loading of these two sentences is striking: the effect is achieved, it seems to me, from the step-by-step subordination, proceeding ever downwards until the sentences seem rather to halt from lack of breath to go farther, than to stop at the conclusion of the statement of an idea.

But this is early, and quite obvious. In her later works she develops a variation on this technique; she constructs sentences 'too elaborate', as Miss Lascelles says, 'for ... [the] powers' of her 'tiresome talkers'.[2] There are, for example, Mr Elton and Mrs Clay, who are much better parodies than Mr Collins because they are more than parodies. Consider, for example, the vicar of Highbury as he reacts to Emma's drawing of Harriet:

'You have made her too tall, Emma,' said Mr Knightley.

Emma knew that she had, but would not own it, and Mr Elton warmly added,

'Oh, no! certainly not too tall; not in the least too tall. Consider, she is sitting down – which naturally presents a different – which in short gives exactly the idea – and the proportions must be preserved, you know. Proportions, foreshortening. – Oh, no! it gives one exactly the idea of such a height as Miss Smith's. Exactly so indeed!'[3]

Mr Elton is stumbling about, trying to find ends for sentences

1. *Pride and Prejudice*, pp. 62, 63.
2. Lascelles, op. cit., p. 89.
3. *Emma*, p. 48.

which he has enough imagination and wind to begin – but which he cannot satisfactorily bring to a conclusion. One thinks, in this connexion, of Miss Bates, whose conversation is far from meaningless. She has, as Miss Lascelles points out, two subtle idiosyncrasies in speech; she 'seldom completes a sentence' and 'each sentence flies off at a tangent from the last, but so characteristic are the trains of thought that, when need is, every sentence elucidates its curtailed predecessor.' Thus Miss Bates says to Emma, '"... upon my word, Miss Woodhouse, you do look – how do you like Jane's hair?"'[1]

Understatement is of course a main aspect of irony; the device used is almost always that of negation – the *New English Dictionary* cites as its example of litotes, 'a citizen of no mean city'. In Jane Austen's works there are hundreds of instances of this kind of irony.

> Mrs Jennings was a widow, with an ample jointure. She had only two daughters, both of whom she had lived to see respectably married, and she had now therefore nothing to do but to marry all the rest of the world.[2]

The sentence reads 'straight' until the last phrase, which brings the reader up short, makes him ponder (and transform) the meaning of the word 'nothing' here – and thus get a glimpse of the triviality of Mrs Jennings's existence in a way that would not be possible were the author to state the facts unironically. The reversal, however, is deceptively simple, for in essence Mrs Jennings is a character ironically perceived: she is a woman who leads a trivial existence, her gossipy curiosity is positively painful, her failure of intelligence leads to a too facile approbation of Willoughby. But her heart is unfailingly kind, and her instinctive generosity stands in clear contrast to the calculating Lucy Steele – even, in fact, to the coldly selfish Lady Middleton. So the reader must be wary of taking ironic remarks and merely holding them up to a mirror.

1. Lascelles, op. cit., pp. 94, 95; *Emma*, p. 323 (cited by Miss Lascelles, p. 95).
2. *Sense and Sensibility*, p. 36.

In dialogue or in letters, the people of whom Jane Austen disapproves sometimes have a penchant for multiple negatives. Thus Willoughby writes to Marianne: 'I shall never reflect on my former acquaintance with your family in Devonshire without the most grateful pleasure, and flatter myself it will not be broken by any mistake or misapprehension of my actions.' [1] This is, on his part, a piece of deliberately nasty understatement: he knows the cruelty which his letter contains; in his conversation with Elinor at the end of the book he admits as much, and though we then learn that the letter was dictated by the young man's indignant fiancée, we do not withhold our disapprobation for his responsibility in the matter. Yet even he, so far as the intention of the book is concerned, is entitled to the forgiveness following upon confession and penance. Again, General Tilney remarks to Catherine: ' "... no endeavours shall be wanting on our side to make Northanger Abbey not wholly disagreeable." ' And William Collins writes: ' "I cannot be otherwise than concerned at being the means of injuring your amiable daughters...." ' [2] Neither of these people is saved by any extenuating characteristic; both are unconscious of the ironies which they so often utter. In the case of the general, this postscript to his invitation to Catherine is but a subtle forewarning of the kind of man he will turn out to be: he is a villain, much more terrifyingly the villain of the piece than John Thorpe, for General Tilney is the agent of Catherine's realization that common sense, of which she is gradually learning the value, is itself limited. And William Collins, while he provides delight not only to Mr Bennet and Elizabeth but to every reader of *Pride and Prejudice*, serves (as we have seen) as the straw which breaks the back of whatever morality Charlotte Lucas possesses.

But Jane Austen also uses this technique for the characters whom she more fully approves. Catherine Morland, for instance, has the following reaction to John Thorpe:

1. ibid., p. 183.

2. *Northanger Abbey*, pp. 139, 140; *Pride and Prejudice*, p. 63. These two cited by Miss Lascelles, op. cit., p. 89.

> Little as Catherine was in the habit of judging for herself, and unfixed as were her general notions of what men ought to be, she could not entirely repress a doubt, while she bore with the effusions of his endless conceit, of his being altogether completely agreeable.[1]

The irony here is wholly exterior to the character portrayed: it is in the point of view that ironic distance is achieved. Catherine tenderly holds in check her native good sense when she must form a judgement of her confidante's brother who is also her own brother's university friend. The multiple negatives are inserted by the narrator, who would subtly underline John Thorpe's fatuity by showing that even the credulous heroine is not beyond judging him adversely. Further than this, the passage helps to measure the distance between Catherine's childish delusions and the good sense which she is later forced to allow to emerge. Again, Fanny Price, after the departure of Maria and Julia from Mansfield, finds her position is improved: '... it was impossible for her not to be more looked at, more thought of and attended to, than she had ever been before.'[2] The understatement here serves several purposes which could emphatically not be made clear were the remark to be made positively. A double judgement is involved – one, of Fanny, who is thus shown hardly able to comprehend the fact of her new importance; the other, of the family at Mansfield, who themselves barely realize that the shift in status has taken place.

In fact, as one moves from the early works into the complexities of *Mansfield Park* and the two succeeding novels, one observes a deepening of Jane Austen's stylistic use of understatement. Of the two Miss Bertrams she writes, '... it is not very wonderful that with all their promising talents and early information, they should be entirely deficient in the less common acquirements of self-knowledge, generosity, and humility.'[3] Here the strength conferred by the negative statement is desirable in order to emphasize what lies at the root

1. *Northanger Abbey*, p. 66.
2. *Mansfield Park*, p. 205.
3. ibid., p. 19.

of their difficulties; in a sense, *Mansfield Park* is (as we have seen) about education. James Rushworth is similarly characterized as 'an inferior young man, as ignorant in business as in books, with opinions in general unfixed, and without seeming much aware of it himself'.[1] Henry Crawford who, however attractive, is always intended by the author as a villain, betrays his own trifling character when he confides in his sister his ambition with regard to Fanny:

> 'I only want her to look kindly on me, to give me smiles as well as blushes, to keep a chair for me by herself wherever we are, and be all animation when I take it and talk to her; to think as I think, be interested in all my possessions and pleasures, try to keep me longer at Mansfield, and feel when I go away that she shall never be happy again. I want nothing more.'[2]

But perhaps subtlest of all is the carefully modulated description of Lady Bertram's reaction to Maria's elopement:

> Lady Bertram did not think deeply, but, guided by Sir Thomas, she thought justly on all important points; and she saw, therefore, in all its enormity, what had happened, and neither endeavoured herself, nor required Fanny to advise her, to think little of guilt and infamy.[3]

It is because of the negatives here that the reader is deeply struck by what has happened to Lady Bertram; this is her moment (the only one she has in the book) of self-awareness, of self-examination; it cannot be violent, because she is morally apathetic – she is one of the main causes of her daughters' defections; but when we untwist the negatives we see through to a most serious, scrutinizing bit of self-knowledge. In order to test the irony of this (and by implication of previous) minor pieces of understatement, let us ask how else Jane Austen might have expressed this thought: she might simply have written, 'Even Lady Bertram was deeply affected.' Then the contrast between her usual phlegmatic behaviour and this quite extraordinary moment would have been made clear – but it would have been far less effective, because, as Jane

1. ibid., p. 200. 2. ibid., p. 231. 3. ibid., p. 449.

Austen writes it, the incident is a projection of Lady Bertram's spirit rather than a cursorily objective remark of the author. But there is no real contradiction involved, even when this sentence is related to the theme of the novel: for the theme itself is not primarily ironic. Thus stylistic irony need not, even in Jane Austen, always be the signal of ambivalent intention, though other valuable purposes may be served.[1]

Without further multiplying examples of understatement, we shall turn to another stylistic device of irony, antiphrasis – that is 'use of words in a sense opposite to their proper meaning' (*N.E.D.*). The sign of antiphrasis is not negation, as in litotes, but of reasonable contradiction in meaning. Of Edward Ferrars, Jane Austen writes: 'All his wishes centered in domestic comfort and the quiet of private life. Fortunately he had a younger brother who was more *promising*.'[2] The italicized word, coming at the end of a long paragraph describing Edward, brings the reader up short, for the plain inference is that the young man's failure to have gaudy ambitions is worthy, and that his mother's desire to see him distinguished in a very worldly way is regrettable. Thus we are prepared to see, in the 'promising' brother, the reverse of Edward: and indeed Robert Ferrars turns out to be vain, selfish, snobbish, stupid. Mrs Ferrars is described with venom:

> ... her features [were] small, without beauty, and naturally without expression; but a *lucky* contraction of the brow had *rescued* her countenance from the *disgrace of insipidity*, by giving it the strong characters of pride and ill nature.[3]

If the reader wonders why he gets such a strong impression of Mrs Ferrars's 'pride and ill nature', he need only re-examine the antiphrasis by which Jane Austen prepares us for these descriptive words. By forcing the words to stand self-contradicted, the author enjoins our attention to a passage which might otherwise be skipped over as conventional description.

1. Compare Forster's remarks on this passage, in *Aspects of the Novel*, pp. 101–4.

2. *Sense and Sensibility*, p. 16.

3. ibid., p. 232.

Throughout *Northanger Abbey* the burlesque element is emphasized by the deliberate misuse of words. Mrs Morland, for example, is 'a woman of useful plain sense, with a good temper, and, what is more *remarkable,* with a good constitution'.[1] It is 'remarkable' for a mother to be these things only in the Gothic novel, which, Jane Austen shows us, is very far removed from actuality.

The Bingley sisters must be set down early as '*very fine ladies;* not deficient in good humour when they were pleased, nor in the power of being agreeable where they chose it; but proud and conceited'.[2] And Charlotte Lucas accepts Mr Collins 'solely from the *pure* and *disinterested* desire of an establishment'.[3] By using these words, Jane Austen does in fact emphasize the impurity and interestedness which lie behind Charlotte Lucas's acceptance of the fatuous clergyman; in making the statement so strongly positive the author underlines the severe moral criticism she is making of Charlotte.

As a final example, let us look at Emma after she has accepted Mr Knightley:

> It is *remarkable,* that Emma, in the many, very many, points of view in which she was now beginning to consider Donwell Abbey, was never struck with any sense of injury to her nephew Henry, whose rights as heir expectant had formerly been so tenaciously regarded.[4]

Jane Austen cannot think this 'remarkable', for she has shown us in the book that Emma's insistence that little Henry have Donwell is but a sign of her self-deception, a symbol of her unconscious love for Mr Knightley. But the author, in using the word here, amusingly reminds us of the distance that her heroine has gone towards knowing herself.

The device of what Miss Lascelles calls 'counterfeit connexion' – 'the deliciously bland appearance of logical connexion' – is an important facet of Jane Austen's style.

1. *Northanger Abbey*, p. 13.
2. *Pride and Prejudice*, p. 15.
3. ibid., p. 122.
4. *Emma*, p. 449.

In her mature work it is not a mere verbal entertainment; we are made to laugh, not at a particular idiosyncrasy which may not happen to be ours, but at the interaction of idiosyncrasy and life.[1]

But this technique does, it seems to me, do more than evoke our laughter; it demonstrates convincingly Jane Austen's awareness of the limitations of common sense: there is always the implied criticism of bad logic, but so is there the emphatic indication that human beings, as they do not judge rationally, cannot be totally grasped by reason alone. Marianne Dashwood has the following impression of John Willoughby:

His name was good, his residence was in their favourite village, and she soon found out that of all manly dresses a shooting-jacket was the most becoming.[2]

It may not be logical for Marianne to approve Willoughby on account of his shooting-jacket (or perhaps to approve shooting-jackets because he wears one) – but this is a natural reaction and cannot be merely laughed off. After the marriage of Edward and Elinor, the young couple 'had in fact nothing to wish for, but the marriage of Colonel Brandon and Marianne, and rather better pasturage for their cows'.[3] Reason cannot yoke these two ideas together; it is rather the unreason of new happiness – and the reduction in perspective it brings – that reduces all wishes to the same level. ' "Well, my dear," Mr Woodhouse says after Mrs Elton's visit, "considering we never saw her before, she seems a very pretty sort of young lady." '[4] We know that reason is not one of Mr Woodhouse's strong points – if we were to judge him for his reason alone, we should have to condemn him; but he has many fine qualities – spontaneous generosity, loyalty, and kindness – which may exist partly *because of* his failure to be quite strictly rational.

Syntactical anti-climax is no new thing in Jane Austen.

1. Lascelles, op. cit., pp. 144, 145.
2. *Sense and Sensibility*, p. 43.
3. ibid., pp. 374, 375.
4. *Emma*, p. 279. Cited by Miss Lascelles, op. cit., p. 144.

One remembers the most famous lines in 'The Vanity of Human Wishes', in which the great 'Swedish Charles' is thus described:

> He left the name at which the world grew pale,
> To point a moral or adorn a tale.

There are many echoes and variations of this device in Jane Austen's novels. John Dashwood 'was not an ill-disposed young man, unless to be rather cold hearted, and rather selfish, is to be ill-disposed'.[1] Thus she indicates by anti-climax the vapidity of the young man. Isabella Thorpe writes to Catherine Morland as follows:

> I am quite uneasy about your dear brother, not having heard from him since he went to Oxford; and am fearful of some misunderstanding. Your kind offices will set all right: – he is the only man I ever did or could love, and I trust you will convince him of it. The spring fashions are partly down; and the hats the most frightful you can imagine.[2]

Here the anti-climax is unintentional on the part of the writer of the letter; and the juxtaposition of her reassertion of love for James with her remarks on the spring fashions only shows that she puts both on the same level, and cannot be quite serious about Catherine's brother. Lydia Wickham, newly married and triumphantly describing her wedding to Elizabeth, says, ' "... I was thinking, you may suppose, of my dear Wickham. I longed to know whether he would be married in his blue coat." '[3] She, like Isabella Thorpe before her, puts love on the same level with fashionable clothing – and so casts doubt on the sincerity and profundity of her ability to love. Finally, when Elizabeth Bennet asks Lady Catherine why she may not accept Darcy, Lady Catherine replies, ' "Because honour, decorum, prudence, nay, interest, forbid it." '[4] Indeed it is 'interest' rather than anything else which makes Lady Catherine so loath to see Darcy and Elizabeth married – a very

1. *Sense and Sensibility*, p. 5.
2. *Northanger Abbey*, p. 216.
3. *Pride and Prejudice*, p. 319.
4. ibid., p. 355.

strong 'interest' that her own daughter shall be her nephew's wife. When, in *Emma*, Mrs Churchill dies,

It was felt as such things must be felt. Everybody had a degree of gravity and sorrow; tenderness towards the departed, solicitude for the surviving friends; and, in a reasonable time, curiosity to know where she would be buried.[1]

Certainly this is anti-climactic, certainly it involves a deliberate criticism of the way people's minds work at such a time – a human descent from sorrow to curiosity, a human contradiction between sympathy and concern with petty matters.

One of the most interesting facts about Jane Austen's style is that it is almost entirely unmetaphorical, except when more or less adverse criticism is meant. Miss Lascelles is, I think, the first critic to make this point; and conjectures that she is '*shy* of figurative language' because of its tendency to become cliché and because 'it cannot *fossilize* without turning into a lie'.[2] There is plenty of evidence to support this conjecture. For instance, Jane Austen writes to Anna about one of the characters in the latter's novel:

Devereux Forester's being ruined by his Vanity is extremely good; but I wish you would not let him plunge into 'a vortex of Dissipation'. I do not object to the Thing, but I cannot bear the expression; – it is such thorough novel slang – and so old, that I dare say Adam met with it in the first novel he opened.[3]

This of course is an animadversion simply on triteness: but a look at Jane Austen's novels will convince the reader that any figurative expression is suspect. Sir John Middleton tells Marianne:

'Poor Brandon! he is quite smitten already, and he is very well worth *setting your cap* at, I can tell you, in spite of all this tumbling about and spraining of ancles.'[4]

The baronet's mode of expression is rather vulgar; he is a

1. *Emma*, p. 387.
2. Lascelles, op. cit., pp. 111, 112. Italics Miss Lascelles's.
3. *Letters*, II, p. 404 (to Anna Austen, 28 September 1814).
4. *Sense and Sensibility*, p. 45.

rather vulgar man – a good and decent neighbour but so unperceptive as to approve Willoughby because the young man rides and shoots well. Intelligence is not his strong suit, and the point is made (in part) by his use of cliché.

Isabella Thorpe says to Catherine Morland, who has not been able to find her confidante at the dance,

'Do go and see for her, Mr Morland, said I – but all in vain – he would not *stir an inch*. ... I have been scolding him to such a degree, my dear Catherine, you would be quite amazed. – You know I never *stand upon ceremony* with such people.' [1]

Behind the façade of fossilized metaphor the reader sees (and partly on account of that metaphor) the insincerity of Isabella. But of course one of the purposes of *Northanger Abbey* is to satirize the Gothic novel; Jane Austen does so by imitating the diction used. Describing Catherine's misery, she writes:

And now I may dismiss my heroine to the sleepless couch, which is the true heroine's portion; to a pillow strewed with thorns and wet with tears.[2]

Catherine *is* miserable – but not about murder or seduction or adultery; she has only been gulled into taking a ride in John Thorpe's carriage. Again, General Tilney finally accedes to the marriage of Henry, his son, and Catherine Morland, largely because of Eleanor's marriage to a rich and important man – 'an accession of dignity that *threw him into a fit of* good-humour, from which he did not recover till after Eleanor had obtained his forgiveness of Henry.' [3]

In *Pride and Prejudice*, Darcy is liked by those in the Netherfield 'neighbourhood' 'till his manners gave a disgust which *turned the tide* of his popularity; for he was discovered to be proud ...',[4] the grandeur of the metaphor reflecting the shallowness of those who eagerly admire him because he is handsome, but quickly reject him when his diffidence or pride makes him seem unresponsive. Mr Collins is, of course, full of

1. *Northanger Abbey*, p. 56. Cf. p. 40.
2. ibid., p. 90.
3. ibid., p. 250. See pp. 71, 79, 89, 98, 113, 187 for other examples.
4. *Pride and Prejudice*, p. 10.

figures. He says in his letter to Mr Bennet that he hopes the latter will not 'reject the offered olive branch', a cliché which even Mary discovers to be '"not wholly new"'. And writing to Mr Bennet after hearing of Lydia's elopement, he says:

> Let me advise you . . . to console yourself as much as possible, to *throw off* your unworthy child from your affection for ever, and leave her to *reap the fruits* of her own heinous offence.[1]

Mary Bennet's reaction is quite as frightening:

> 'This is a most unfortunate affair; and will probably be much talked of. But we must *stem the tide* of malice, and *pour into* the *wounded bosoms* of each other, the *balm* of sisterly consolation.'[2]

Here the effect – or perhaps the cause – of fossilized thinking takes a nasty turn; and there is nastiness as well behind Lady Catherine de Bourgh's famous mixed metaphor on the prospect of Elizabeth's marriage to Darcy: '"Heaven and earth! – of what are you thinking? Are the *shades* of Pemberley to be thus *polluted*?"'[3]

Mansfield Park also contains figurative language, again in the speech of the characters we are meant to dislike. Mrs Norris says, of Fanny: '"Is not she a sister's child? and could I bear to see her want, while I had a bit of bread to give her?"'[4] This is intended by the speaker to be a rhetorical question – but to the experienced reader of Jane Austen the answer must be yes: and the remainder of the novel shows just how regardless Mrs Norris can be of her niece's welfare or happiness. Again, Mary Crawford says: '"A large income is the best *recipé* for happiness I ever heard of. It certainly may secure all the *myrtle* and *turkey part* of it.'[5] This figure, like her actions generally, betrays the flippancy and selfishness of the character of the girl.

1. *Pride and Prejudice*, pp. 63, 64, 297.
2. ibid., p. 289. See also pp. 67, 140 for other examples.
3. ibid., p. 357.
4. *Mansfield Park*, p. 7. Quoted by Miss Lascelles, op. cit., p. 112. See *Mansfield Park*, pp. 29, 189 for other examples of Aunt Norris's egregious metaphors.
5. ibid., p. 213.

In *Emma*, Mrs Elton asserts of her husband, '"he was sure at this rate it would be May before *Hymen's saffron robe* would be put on for us!"' And the same lady expresses her pleasure at the 'situation' she has found for Jane Fairfax: 'Delightful, charming, superior, first *circles, spheres, lines, ranks,* every thing....' [1]

This technique is again used in *Persuasion* to disclose thin thinking. Thus Lady Russell is all too ready to change her mind about William Walter Elliot when he comes to Bath. 'If he really sought to reconcile himself like a dutiful *branch*, he must be forgiven for having *dismembered* himself from the paternal *tree*.' [2] It is rather Lady Russell's inordinate respect for rank than any very good sense which prompts this willingness to forgive him. She is wrong; he is even more of a villain than she has previously thought him to be; and I suggest that this unlovely figure of speech is a subtle preparation for the disclosure of his true nature. There is also, in *Persuasion*, one small sign of the direction in which Jane Austen might have developed had she not died so young. Mrs Smith tells Anne the truth about William Walter Elliot:

> 'He is totally beyond the reach of any sentiment of justice or compassion. Oh! he is *black at heart, hollow and black*!' [3]

Since Mrs Smith is a 'good' character, and since this exclamation comes at the end of an impassioned and deeply felt denunciation of Mr Elliot, we must infer that this figure of speech is not meant to be taken ironically. Two possibilities lie open: as is well known, *Persuasion* was not completely revised before Jane Austen's death, and the author may simply have omitted to excise this metaphor; or, second, she may have come to trust metaphor in her last more or less finished composition. The problem can never be settled, no doubt, but at least it is not altogether unlikely that Jane Austen would have moved towards figurative language had she lived.

This remark brings up the whole general question of

1. *Emma*, pp. 308, 359. 2. *Persuasion*, p. 136. 3. ibid., p. 199.

development in Jane Austen's prose style. H. W. Garrod, in asserting that *Pride and Prejudice* is Jane Austen's masterpiece, says that 'Jane Austen could write at twenty as well, or better, or very nearly as well, as at forty'.[1] Quite aside from the fact that this statement ignores the vexed problem of chronology in the Austen canon, it does (I think) ignore as well the changed tone of the works which are known to be late – *Mansfield Park, Emma,* and *Persuasion.* In 1813, she looks back on *Pride and Prejudice* with the following shrewd comment:

> The work is rather too light, and bright, and sparkling; it wants shade; it wants to be stretched out here and there with a long chapter of sense, if it could be had; if not, of solemn specious nonsense, about something unconnected with the story; an essay on writing, a critique on Walter Scott, or the history of Buonaparté, or anything that would form a contrast, and bring the reader with increased delight to the playfulness and epigrammatism of the general style.[2]

Behind the playfulness of this paragraph is, I think, a genuine recognition that variation in tone is necessary. It can be found, it seems to me, in all three of the later works – in *Mansfield Park* and *Persuasion* obviously, but in *Emma* too, especially in the heroine's moments of self-awareness, which have nothing playful about them.

'I doubt', says Dr Chapman, 'if J. A. was conscious of having a style of her own. Outside her dialogue it is not highly individual; it is just the ordinary correct English that, as Johnson had said, "everyone now writes".'[3] I believe he underrates her on this point. It seems to me fully apparent that Jane Austen is as thoroughly original (or 'new', in Eliot's sense) in her style as she is in the other aspects of her work. Indeed, as Bacon told us long ago, style cannot be regarded as a peripheral matter. Like her literary forebears she uses stylistic devices (even including those usually associated with the term 'irony') for many purposes, both ironic and un-ironic – from

1. H. W. Garrod, 'Jane Austen: a Depreciation', p. 28.
2. *Letters*, II, pp. 299, 300 (to Cassandra Austen, 4 February 1813).
3. R. W. Chapman, *Jane Austen Facts and Problems*, p. 209.

mere delightful *jeux d'esprit* to solemn considered judgements.

Language as the raw material of literature imposes upon the artist certain rules which cannot be safely transgressed; the writer, dependent upon a tradition, cannot wholly disregard it. Even Gertrude Stein's automatic writing is deeply founded upon a linguistic history; her failure is not in departing altogether, but in veering too far, from the requirements of diction and syntax.[1] Language and its principles are in a sense the shadow which falls between the creative impulse and the work of art. On the other hand, language, having a logic of its own, can (as we have seen) disclose that of which the artist may be only vaguely aware – or of which he may be quite unconscious: *'Et l'ayant dit,'* writes Claudel, *'je sais ce que j'ai dit.'*[2] So language – like clay or paint – is a transfiguring material, not a lens through which the artist projects his vision. But, unlike clay or paint, language is a human instrument, a human achievement with a human structure – and is therefore both intrinsically and potentially expressive of the contradictions of man's heart and mind. It is for this reason that literature is more adequate than any other art form to ironic expression.

So far as style is concerned, it has been the purpose of this chapter to show that Jane Austen's irony is much more pervasive than the usual rhetorical categories will allow. Understatement and antiphrasis by no means account for all the ironies in her diction and syntax. But other categories – however useful in an analysis of this kind – betray their own inadequacies at the moment when the light thus shed reveals farther, deeper, subtler shadows: for style, more perhaps than any other aspect of a novel, is a finally indissoluble unity, a fabric which cannot be cut up without destroying the harmony of the whole. It is because of this fact that such difficult but useful words as 'tone' and 'texture' are so often applied to

1. As E. M. Forster remarks in *Aspects of the Novel*, pp. 60, 61.

2. Paul Claudel, *La Ville*, quoted by E. M. Forster, 'The *Raison d'Être* of Criticism in the Arts', in *Two Cheers for Democracy*, p. 115.

style. And, however difficult it may be to analyse the whole style of a lyric poem, the task is plainly impossible in a novel – unless one is willing to read perhaps a thousand pages of explication; and this is no doubt more trouble than it is worth. One recourse, and it is a pleasant one, is to read the novels themselves, bearing in mind the 'transparent vesture' (as Thirlwall says in another connexion) which, as much perhaps as anything else, is responsible for Jane Austen's front rank among the English novelists.

ANNOTATED BIBLIOGRAPHY

BIBLIOGRAPHIES

Two bibliographies of Jane Austen appear annually in *Philological Quarterly*, one in the April issue, in 'The Romantic Movement: a Selective and Critical Bibliography', the other in the July issue, in 'English Literature 1660–1800: a Current Bibliography'. These should be used to bring up to date the bibliographies listed below.

Stephen, George Arthur, 'Austen Centenary, a Bibliography', Norwich Public Library's *Readers' Guide*, VI (June 1917), 40–3. Now entirely superseded by the more recent bibliographies listed here.

Edmonds, Jean Lowrie, 'Jane Austen: Biography and Criticism', *Bulletin of Bibliography*, XII (1925), 129–34. Full of inaccuracies but contains many bibliographical references, particularly American, which Keynes does not include.

Keynes, Geoffrey Langdon, *Jane Austen: a Bibliography*, London, 1929. Particularly valuable on the early editions, but spotty in its periodical listings.

Tallmadge, Abby Louise, *Sense and Sensibility: Austenian Gleanings*, Diss. (unpublished), Northwestern University, 1935. A thoroughgoing source study of *Sense and Sensibility*, together with a first-rate annotated bibliography.

Mudrick, Marvin, *The Achievement of Jane Austen: a Study in Ironic Process*, Diss. (published without bibliography as *Jane Austen: Irony as Defense and Discovery*, Princeton, 1952), University of California (Berkeley), 1949. Brings Edmonds and Keynes up to date.

Chapman, Robert William, *Jane Austen: a Critical Bibliography*, 2nd ed., Oxford, 1955. Indispensable, but extremely sketchy on secondary sources.

Link, Frederick Martin, *The Reputation of Jane Austen in the Twentieth Century, with an Annotated Enumerative Bibliography of Austen Criticism from 1811 to June, 1957*, Diss. (unpublished), Boston University, 1958. Indispensable and although unpublished can be obtained on microfilm or Xerox.

LETTERS

The Chapman edition of Jane Austen's letters is the most complete and the most accurate, but I list the others as well, because they may occasionally be more readily available.

Austen-Leigh, James Edward, *A Memoir of Jane Austen*, London, 1870,

2nd ed., 1871. This memoir (see page 197 below) contains the first collection of Jane Austen's letters, but Mr Austen-Leigh had access only to the letters belonging to his branch of the family.

Brabourne, Edward Hugessen Knatchbull, *Baron*, ed., *Letters of Jane Austen*, London, 1884. The son of Jane Austen's niece Fanny Knight, Lord Brabourne had access to another group of letters, which he published virtually in their entirety.

Austen-Leigh, William and Richard Arthur, *Jane Austen: Her Life and Letters: a Family Record*, London, 1913. Drawing upon both the above authorities, and upon the various manuscripts at their disposal, Messrs Austen-Leigh had, however, as 'no part of their plan to edit the letters as a whole. Almost every extant letter is quoted by them, but relatively few are given entire' (Chapman, ed., *Letters*, I, v).

Chapman, Robert William, ed., *Jane Austen's Letters to Her Sister Cassandra and Others*, 2nd ed., Oxford, 1952. Based on all previous authorities, manuscript and printed, this edition is the best. A selection from these was made by Dr Chapman for the World's Classics edition of 1955.

FRAGMENTS, ETC.

All the fragments have now been collected and published as *The Works of Jane Austen: Volume VI: Minor Works*, ed. Robert William Chapman, London, 1954.

Austen, Jane, *Volume the First*, ed. Robert William Chapman, Oxford, 1933. The first book of juvenilia.

Love and Freindship and Other Early Works, London, 1922. Contains 'Love and Freindship' (1790); 'Lesley Castle'; 'The History of England' (1791); a collection of letters; scraps.

Lady Susan, ed. Robert William Chapman, Oxford, 1925. Written about 1805, 'Lady Susan' was first published in 1871, in the second edition of the Austen-Leigh *Memoir of Jane Austen*.

The Watsons, ed. Robert William Chapman, Oxford, 1927. Written perhaps before 'Lady Susan' (see Chapman, *Jane Austen Facts and Problems*, p. 163), this fragment also appeared in the 1871 edition of the *Memoir*.

Plan of a Novel According to Hints from Various Quarters, ed. Robert William Chapman, Oxford, 1926. Dr Chapman conjectures that this was written about 1816.

Sanditon, ed. Robert William Chapman, Oxford, 1925. This is Jane Austen's last composition, written between January and March 1817.

Three Evening Prayers, San Francisco, 1940.

THE NOVELS

The early editions of Jane Austen's novels are accorded thorough treatment in the Keynes bibliography, which contains not only all essential information but facsimiles of title-pages of both the English and French editions. Dr Chapman's bibliography supplements that of Keynes. At present there are many usable editions of the novels. For reasons set forth below I list only that edited by Dr Chapman.

Chapman, Robert William, ed., *The Novels of Jane Austen, the Text Based on Collation of the Early Editions, with Notes, Indexes and Illustrations from Contemporary Sources*, 5 vols., 3rd ed., Oxford, 1933. Although the Chapman text is now used – though not widely enough – in certain other editions, this is the first and best scholarly edition of the six novels, and one of its many perfections is the unobtrusiveness of the scholarship. Besides, Dr Chapman is a sensitive critic. These volumes are accordingly not only the most attractive available but the most authoritative; and there are many additional features – illustrations, notes on the text, discussions of Jane Austen's syntax, of the customs of the period, and so forth. The illustrations are particularly fine.

BIOGRAPHY AND CRITICISM – BOOKS

In this and the following sections I have been highly selective; the keys to an exhaustive bibliography are contained on page 195 above. I have listed many standard commentaries, good and bad, because they are often referred to and need annotation. Furthermore, I have included reference to remarks by representative literary figures, even if the remarks are fragmentary, for I feel that what one writer says of another is of special interest. Finally, I have included one or two critical curiosities because they show something of the byways of Jane Austen criticism.

Apperson, George Latimer, *A Jane Austen Dictionary*, London, 1932. An index of characters.

Austen-Leigh, James Edward, *A Memoir of Jane Austen*, 2nd ed., London, 1871. This is preferable to the first edition because it contains 'Lady Susan' and 'The Watsons'. See next entry.

A Memoir of Jane Austen, ed. Robert William Chapman, Oxford, 1926. 'A reprint of the second edition (1871) omitting the sketches, Lady Susan, and The Watsons.' Dr Chapman's edition has the disadvantage of not containing these fragments, but the advantage of notes and an index.

Austen-Leigh, William and Richard Arthur, *Jane Austen, Her Life and Letters, a Family Record*, London, 1913. Like the *Memoir*, this work is of first importance to any Jane Austen biographer: all subsequent biographies have been based almost entirely on these two works.

Bailey, John Cann, *Introductions to Jane Austen*, London, 1931. Dependable but dull.

Bowen, Elizabeth, 'Jane Austen', in Derek Verschoyle, ed., *The English Novelists*, New York, 1936, 101–13. Although this piece is in the main illuminating, its insistence on Jane Austen's 'unperplexity' is strange.

Bradley, Andrew Cecil, 'Jane Austen', in *Essays and Studies by Members of the English Association*, II (1911), 7–36. 'There are two distinct strains in Jane Austen. She is a moralist and a humorist' – and in many respects resembles Dr Johnson. Bradley, I think, rather overdoes the connexion to Johnson.

Brontë, Charlotte, *The Brontës: Life and Letters*, by Clement King Shorter, 2 vols., London, 1908. See the letters to George Henry Lewes, I, 387, 388 (12 and 18 January 1848); and the letter to W. S. Williams, II, 127, 128 (12 April 1850). A famous dissent on Jane Austen, whom Charlotte Brontë finds accurate and apt, but commonplace and lacking in fire.

Brower, Reuben Arthur, 'Light and Bright and Sparkling: Irony and Fiction in *Pride and Prejudice*', in *The Shores of Light*, New York, 1951, 164–81. An excellent stylistic study.

Browning, Elizabeth Barrett, *The Letters of Elizabeth Barrett Browning*, ed. Frederic G. Kenyon, 2 vols., New York, 1897. See the letter to Ruskin, II, 217 (5 November 1855). '[Miss Mitford] never taught me anything but a very limited admiration of Miss Austen, whose people struck me as wanting souls, even more than is necessary for men & women of the world. The novels are perfect as far as they go – that's certain. Only they don't go far, I think. It may be my fault.'

Cecil, (Lord) David, *Jane Austen* (the Leslie Stephen lecture, 1935), Cambridge, 1936. Literate, perceptive, agreeable, though occasionally redolent.

Chapman, Robert William, *Jane Austen Facts and Problems*, 3rd ed., Oxford, 1950. Indispensable for the scholar, too fragmentary for anyone else.

Child, Harold H., 'Jane Austen', in the *Cambridge History of English Literature*, XII, 257–71. Sane, balanced, and, on the whole, correct.

Coleridge, Sara, *Memoirs and Letters*, ed. by her daughter, 2 vols., London, 1873. See the letter to Emily Trevenen, I, 75 (August 1834). She tells how Wordsworth, Coleridge, and Southey reacted to Jane Austen, the last two favourably; Wordsworth found her lacking in imagination.

Edgeworth, Maria, *Life and Letters*, ed. A. J. C. Hare, 2 vols., Boston, 1895. See the letter to Mrs Ruxton, I, 260 (21 February 1818). Admires *Persuasion*, except the 'tangled, useless histories of the family in the first fifty pages'. Thinks *Northanger Abbey* satisfactory except for General Tilney.

Forster, Edward Morgan, *Abinger Harvest*, London, 1936. See pp. 145–59. The essays on Jane Austen here are disappointingly oblique. *Aspects of the Novel*, London, 1927. Excellent on Lady Bertram, 101–4.

Howells, William Dean, *Heroines of Fiction*, 2 vols., London, 1901. See I, 37–78. Shrewd and idiosyncratic appraisals of all the Jane Austen heroines, all of whom Howells admires.

Jenkins, Elizabeth, *Jane Austen, a Biography*, London, 1938. There is nothing here which cannot be found in, or inferred from, the *Memoir* or the *Life and Letters*, but this work is concise and readable. The biographical section of Miss Lascelles's book is, however, preferable.

Kaye-Smith, Sheila, and Gladys Bronwyn Stern, *Talking of Jane Austen*, London, 1943. This book, like its successor (*More Talk of Jane Austen*, London, 1950), contains insights of interest and perhaps of value, but I find the idolatrous atmosphere daunting.

Kipling, Rudyard, 'The Janeites', in *Debits and Credits*, London, 1926, 157–95. The celebrated story about a cockney mess-waiter whose officers persuade him, under some pressure, to read Jane Austen.

Lascelles, Mary, *Jane Austen and Her Art*, London, 1939. See my Acknowledgement, p. 9.

Macaulay, Thomas Babington, *The Life and Works of Lord Macaulay*, 10 vols., London, 1866. See VII, 42. Puts Jane Austen next to Shakespeare.

McKillop, Alan D., 'Critical Realism in *Northanger Abbey*', in Robert C. Rathburn and Martin Steinmann, Jr, eds., *From Jane Austen to Joseph Conrad*, Minneapolis, 1958, 35–45.

'The context of *Sense and Sensibility*', in *Rice Institute Pamphlets*, XLIV (1957), 65–78. Considers novels Jane Austen read.

Mudrick, Marvin, *Jane Austen: Irony as Defense and Discovery*, Princeton, 1952. See my Acknowledgement, p. 9.

Murrah, Charles, 'The Background of *Mansfield Park*', in Robert C. Rathburn and Martin Steinmann, Jr, eds., *From Jane Austen to Joseph Conrad*, Minneapolis, 1958, 23–34. An important essay which considers the 'sets and props' of the novel.

Read, Herbert, *English Prose Style*, London, 1928. Basing his argument on a misinterpretation of a scene in *Persuasion* Sir Herbert alleges that Jane Austen's style is inadequate to 'the strain of dramatic action' (p. 119).

Scott, Walter, *The Journal of Sir Walter Scott*, 2 vols., Edinburgh, 1890. See I, 155 (14 March 1826); II, 37 (18 September 1827). The first entry is the famous one in which he says he has re-read *Pride and*

Prejudice for 'at least' the third time; that he can do the 'Big Bow-wow strain' himself, but that she excels him in 'the exquisite touch'. See also below.

Spurgeon, Caroline F. E., 'Jane Austen', in *Essays by Divers Hands, being the Transactions of the Royal Society of Literature*, VII (1927), 81–104. Jane Austen is 'characteristically English' and like Shakespeare in some respects. A disappointing piece from so distinguished a scholar.

Tallmadge, Abby Louise, *Sense and Sensibility: Austenian Gleanings*, Diss. (unpublished), Northwestern University, 1935. See page 195 above.

Tennyson, Alfred, *A Memoir by His Son*, 2 vols., London, 1897. Jane Austen's realism is 'nearest to ... Shakespeare', though the latter is 'a sun to which Jane Austen, tho' a bright and true little world, is but an asteroid' (II, 372).

Trilling, Lionel, 'Mansfield Park', in *The Opposing Self*, London, 1955, 206–30. A landmark in Jane Austen criticism. See also page 202 below.

Villard, Léonie, *Jane Austen: a French Appreciation*, trans. by Veronica Lucas, New York, 1924. An inadequate translation of an intelligent, if not quite thoroughly organized, study of Jane Austen's works.

Warner, Sylvia Townsend, *Jane Austen* (Bibliographical Series of Supplements to 'British Book News'), London, 1951. Sensitive, thoughtful, and short.

Woolf, Virginia, 'Jane Austen', in *The Common Reader*, London, 1925, 191–206. Jane Austen as a moralist and as a stylist.

ARTICLES IN PERIODICALS

Some articles printed or reprinted in book form appear alphabetically by author in the preceding section.

[Scott, Walter] 'Emma', *Quarterly Review*, XIV (1815), 188–201. The famous review. Praises the 'neatness and point' of her narratives, but thinks she is sometimes too minutely detailed – and in these circumstances her boring characters (e.g., Miss Bates) bore the reader.

[Whateley, Richard (Archbishop), review of *Northanger Abbey* and *Persuasion*] *Quarterly Review*, XXIV (1821), 352–76. Another famous review. Here Jane Austen is hailed as a novelist whose realism marks a new direction in fiction.

Lewes, George Henry, 'The Novels of Jane Austen', *Blackwood's*, LXXXVI (1859), 99–113. An introduction to Jane Austen by an admirer who would have her more widely known. She is superb, he says, in her characterizations, and in her manner of telling a story, but her themes limit her.

Farrer, Reginald, 'Jane Austen', *Quarterly Review*, CCXXVIII (1917), 1–30. A centenary piece which echoes Macaulay in setting Jane Austen next to Shakespeare on account of their 'common capacity for intense vitalization'. An excellent essay, touching on many matters of critical importance.

[Chapman, Robert William] 'Jane Austen's Methods', *Times Literary Supplement*, 9 February 1922, 81, 82. A fine essay covering many topics of interest – Jane Austen's reading, its application to the novels; the chronology of the canon; chronology within *Pride and Prejudice*; Jane Austen's materials and their alleged limitations.

Garrod, H. W., 'Jane Austen: a Depreciation', in *Transactions of the Royal Society of Literature*, n.s., VIII (1928). Jane Austen is competent but not great. Her novels show that she is interested in manners, but not the human heart. As a writer she is ignorant; her ideals are humdrum; her style is no more than apt. See next entry.

Chapman, Robert William, 'Jane Austen: a Reply to Mr Garrod', in *Transactions of the Royal Society of Literature*, n.s., X (1931). A stinging reply in which among other things Dr Chapman points out that Professor Garrod is not very closely acquainted with Jane Austen's novels.

Harding, D. W., 'Regulated Hatred: an Aspect of the Work of Jane Austen', *Scrutiny*, VIII (1940), 346–62. An iconoclastic and influential essay.

Kliger, Samuel, 'Jane Austen's *Pride and Prejudice* in the Eighteenth-Century Mode', *University of Toronto Quarterly*, XVI (1947), 357–70. 'The antithesis between art and nature is the "governing idea" in *Pride and Prejudice*': Elizabeth represents 'nature' and Darcy 'art'.

Daiches, David, 'Jane Austen, Karl Marx, and the Aristocratic Dance', *American Scholar*, XVII (1948), 289–96. Jane Austen is 'the only English novelist of stature who was in a sense a Marxist before Marx'. In what sense?

Schorer, Mark, 'Fiction and the "Matrix of Analogy"', *Kenyon Review*, XI (1949), 539–60. An attempt to show that the 'dominant metaphorical quality' of *Persuasion* is economic. Professor Schorer's argument, though heavily buttressed, remains a piece of special pleading.

Bradbrook, Frank W., 'Style and Judgment in Jane Austen's Novels', *Cambridge Journal*, IV (1950–51), 515–37. Thoughtful and bold, though sometimes too insistently anti-historical.

Bush, Douglas, 'Mrs Bennet and the Dark Gods: the Truth about Jane Austen', *Sewanee Review*, LXIV (1956), 591–6. A spoof of myth-criticism.

Schorer, Mark, 'Pride Unprejudiced', *Kenyon Review*, XVIII (1956), 72–91. Economics again plays a dominant role in Professor Schorer's argument.

Shannon, Edgar F., Jr, '*Emma:* Character and Construction', *PMLA*, LXXI (1956), 637–50. President Shannon here cogently presents the case that in *Emma* Jane Austen 'has accomplished the hazardous feat of portraying and resolving disharmony entirely from within the heroine herself'.

Trilling, Lionel, 'Emma', *Encounter*, VIII (June 1957), 49–59. First-class, but not up to the standard of his essay on *Mansfield Park*. See preceding section.

Babb, Howard S., 'Dialogue with Feeling: a Note on *Pride and Prejudice*', *Kenyon Review*, XX (1958), 203–16. Analyses Jane Austen's 'management of conversations'.

INDEX